# THE GOOD APPLE GUIDE TO LEARNING CENTERS

**by**

**Craig & Michele Borba**

*Illustrated by*

Nancee Volpe
Stan Lelm
Sandra Zawadzki

ISBN #0-916456-33-1

**Good Apple**
A Division of Frank Schaffer Publications, Inc.
23740 Hawthorne Boulevard
Torrance, CA 90505-5927


Published September 1978.

# TABLE OF CONTENTS

# PREFACE

*I hear and I forget*

*I see and I remember*

*I do and I understand*

—Ancient Chinese Proverb

Craig and I began to use centers several years ago in our classrooms. Both of us are game and task oriented, always enjoying making up new game ideas and activities to use in our rooms. We soon found that we needed a way to organize our steadily-growing materials. Often we would teach a concept, only to find the next week, an activity that would have been so appropriate to the previous lesson. The center approach became a convenient way to organize and incorporate these materials into our daily teaching plan.

We received an added bonus in the process. Not only had we stumbled upon an organizational method we were comfortable with, but also we discovered that our students were delighted with the approach. We noticed an interesting fact occurring in our rooms. Not only did the children seem more interested in the same lessons we were presenting, but they also were learning more. This was supported by looking at their post-test results. The noise level in the room was slightly up, but the noise was now a busy, productive kind of noise, with all the children working on tasks.

The real "selling point" occurred during our daily class meeting evaluation times. Children came back to report learning discoveries they had made during center time that were at times quite profound. The enthusiasm in their voices as they described their experiences of the day were reinforcing enough to make up for the extra time involved. Children were leaving school at dismissal time, and entering the door first thing in the morning, with comments such as: "When can we work in the centers?" and "What's the new center for this week?"

Centers in our rooms were developed gradually. We began each year with one new subject emphasis, so that by the end of a few years, we finally were able to individualize our rooms in all areas. Children who needed to work at a slower pace were now able to; children who needed review and reinforcement in particular concepts could get the appropriate help, and other children who could accelerate, did.

Through our own experiences of working with children in the center setting, we became strongly committed to the belief that children learn best if they are allowed to be active participants in their own learning. The center enables the child to capitalize on all the experiences that are possible in the classroom. The child is able to absorb information through the manipulation of the activities and materials we provide. Each new discovery adds to the child's previous framework of knowledge. How much more exciting it is for us to discover something on our own than being told. And, how much better we remember it!

Each child is a very precious human being with an overwhelming amount of potential. We feel the organization and tasks in this book will aid the teacher in meeting the needs of his or her students as they work towards their individual potentials.

# INTRODUCTION

# INTRODUCTION

By picking up this book you must think centers are interesting in the classroom. You might have had a mind-boggling experience with centers in the past and become discouraged. This book will help you to set up the centers, structure your room, and keep track of your student's progress. It will enable you to individualize and increase your student's learning proficiency. It will also help to increase your children's image of school as a fun and successful place to be. Your classroom structure can easily be changed to the center format. It mainly requires organization and your own commitment to the belief that children learn more from their own active participation with the subject content, than from being told by you.

Where do you fit in this learning environment and what are your responsibilities? The center concept will allow you a greater amount of freedom within your classroom. It will give you more flexibility in subject content, ability ranges, and in time scheduling. It will also put you in a whole new relationship with your students. You will become an active learning partner with your students, helping them make new discoveries, and helping you discover new facts about your students. You might find out that the same child you thought was so turned off by science, loves to observe the behavior of the fish, or the little boy who hates to write, will write volumes about dinosaurs. You'll have time now to enjoy watching your students learn how to learn. By controlling and structuring the environment, you control the basics of what is being learned. The child extends the learning process.

As children explore and experiment, many inner questions develop which aid in extending the learning projects -- many questions that teachers never think of. The opportunity for spontaneous learning and discovery, gives each child a successful learning experience, as well as the thrill of seeing what's behind new doors. As the child begins to view himself as a successful learner, he begins to develop a good concept of his role in school. With guidance, the child will be able to capitalize on his own learning strengths and move ahead at his own pace. The final verdict to the question, "Why the center?", will be the golden moment when the child gaily skips up to you and exclaims, "Can we do it again tomorrow?"

# CENTERS. . . . CENTERS. . . . CENTERS

1. Centers can focus on any topic. Many subjects we, as adults, rule out as uninteresting, are most interesting to a child. Don't exclude anything. Allow students to make their own suggestions.
2. Centers are designed, to provide for the children, active discoveries concerning the topic. Manipulative activities should be plentiful. Children learn by touching and experimenting. Be sure to include lots of things to feel and explore.
3. The opportunity to share ideas with other children also should be part of the center arrangement. Children learn from each other. They need the time to interchange ideas and receive feedback from peers. Exchanging ideas also allows vocabulary enhancement.
4. Centers also are a time for extending learning. The center is designed to introduce the child to a topic, and spark an interest in the subject. Children should be encouraged and helped to pursue topic beyond the activities provided in the classroom, especially if interest is shown.
5. Centers should integrate all subject areas to be totally effective as a learning tool. Even though the purpose of a center is to improve creative writing, be sure to include math, reading, spelling, and art.
6. Topic involvement need not remain only at the center area. Small-group and large-group activities also should be part of the curriculum! Include stories, films, dramatizations, field trips, sharing from home, and arts and crafts.

# CENTER WAYS

There are numerous ways to use the center in the classroom. Each way, though different in its scheduling technique, is similar in that it allows the child the opportunity to work at tasks using the experience method of learning. Variety is the spice of life. Children, in particular, need a chance to experience change. Centers provide that opportunity by allowing children to work and experience a different classroom framework and, therefore, the chance to become aware of their own actions in a different setting. Here are a few approaches to centers:

PROGRAM CARD — Children frequently begin the morning in a group meeting. On a program card, each child decides where he/she will begin his work. Basically, each child plans his/her own schedule.

OPEN CHOICE — Each child is free to move from one center to another center on his/her own. Teachers assist children in making their center selections.

SMALL GROUP ROTATION — The teacher groups the class into small groups (approximately the same in each group). Each group works at a center task together. At a determined signal by the teacher, each group rotates to the next center task.

MULTI-STATIONS — Students are involved in a wide variety of activities set up in the room for a short period of time (example: 3-5 minutes). The activities consist of a number of different tasks, which the participants rotate to and from, at a specified time.

CLASS CENTER SCHEDULE — The teacher begins the center period with a class meeting where the center schedule is explained. Children move from center to center as they complete each task, according to the schedule. The schedule may be written on the blackboad, chart, or on individual cards for each child to use.

ENRICHMENT CENTERS — Children move from center to center as they complete their assigned work tasks. The teacher may assign certain children to work at a center for reinforcement, review of a concept, or for enrichment.

# THE ROOM ENVIRONMENT

Space becomes a new and important dimension as centers are implemented in your classroom. The center format allows new creativity for the teacher to pursue. Large space, formerly used by desks and chairs, can now accommodate pillows, boxes, bookcases, and large tables. The teacher will be challenged many times with the problem, "Where will I find the space?"

Centers need not take up the entire room. You may find it more appropriate to have one large center area in the back of the room or along a side wall. Your children may move to this area when they complete basic work. The beauty of the center concept is the freedom it allows the teacher. Tomorrow may bring the need for an entirely new arrangement, one that is more appropriate to a new center's topics and objectives. Be creative! Try partitioning a few corners with a screen, bookcase, or piano back, to form an activity area. With just a few changes, your whole room can take on a new perspective!

Look around your house, garage, variety stores, and garage sales for things that will make your room look comfortable and functional. Rugs, plants, and rocking chairs always add that "lived in" look that helps to create a warm environment.

Your students can be very helpful in changing your room. Appoint them as "honorary decorating experts" and watch the results! Your class can have pillowmaking parties by stitching around donated material. Stuff large rags and towels inside if you are short on other material.

Rugs can be donated by parents, or can be made by gluing or taping carpet samples together on a large piece of old material.

Old bookcases or crates, pushed together, make excellent dividers for a center. Boards stacked with large bricks also make quick and easy game and book storage areas.

Old paint easels also can be converted to room dividers easily. A center task to be used by children can be hung on the easel.

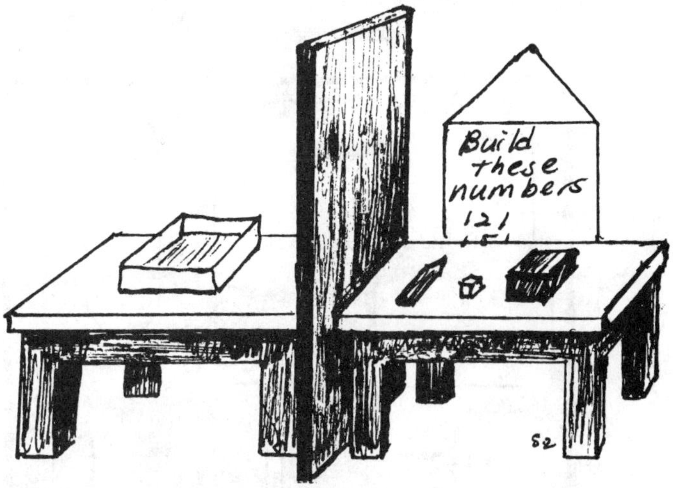


Plywood or chipboard, cut the dimensions of a table, can be used as a divider between two desks. A small center can be arranged on each desk.

The back of a piano can be covered with burlap or chipboard to make another center. The back of a piano also can be used as an excellent room divider.

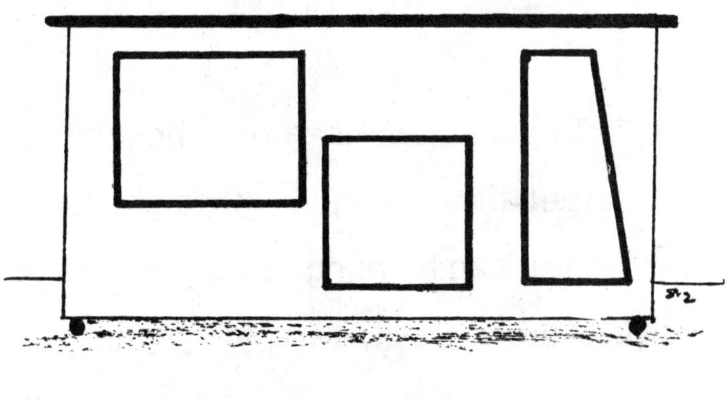

An old movie screen makes a good space divider. Children can finger-paint on it or display their best stories or paintings on it.

A large cardboard crate can be adapted to meet many needs. By placing it upright in the room, a center can be made on each side. If the crate is large enough, create another center inside.

Cutting off one side of a box will create an "office" area inside, where a child can work. Small desks can be placed around the outside of the box to create additional centers.

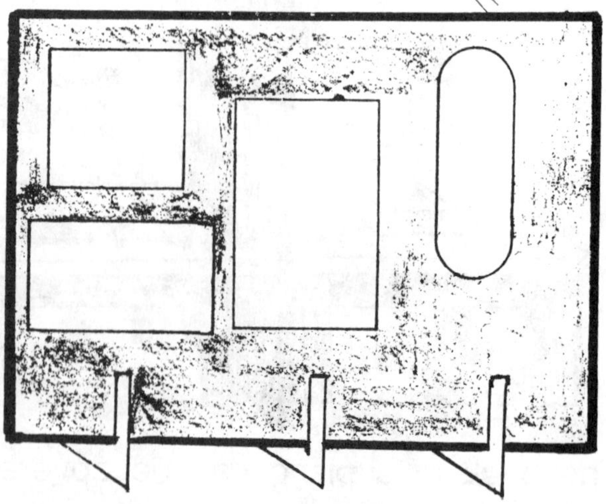

Chart holders also can be functional dividers to the classroom environment. Do not forget the ceiling. Lightweight dividers (paper, cloth, foil, plastic, oilcloth, cardboard) can be hung. Stretch a wire across the room. Use curtains, sheets, and yards of fabric for dividers.

The top of a round table can be sectioned with cardboard into four work areas. Cut two long pieces of cardboard, each the length of the table. Mark the middle point of each piece and slit it almost half way. Turn the pieces so they will intersect each other. Slide together along the cut portions. Position on the center of the table. Hold in place with strips of masking tape.

A cardboard box turned on its side with the top cut off, also can function as a table top office area. Tasks can be attached with clothespins or paper clips to the back and sides of the box.

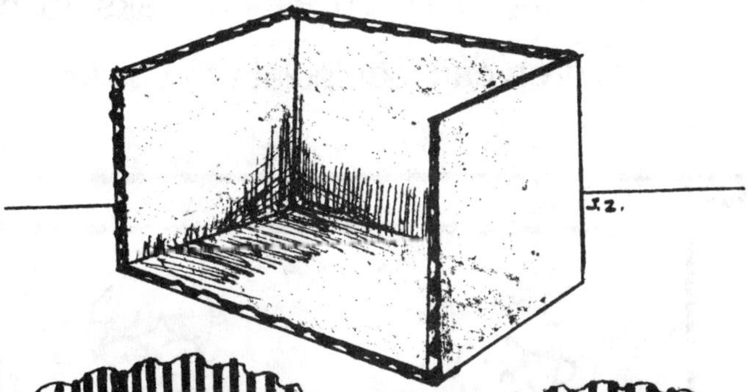

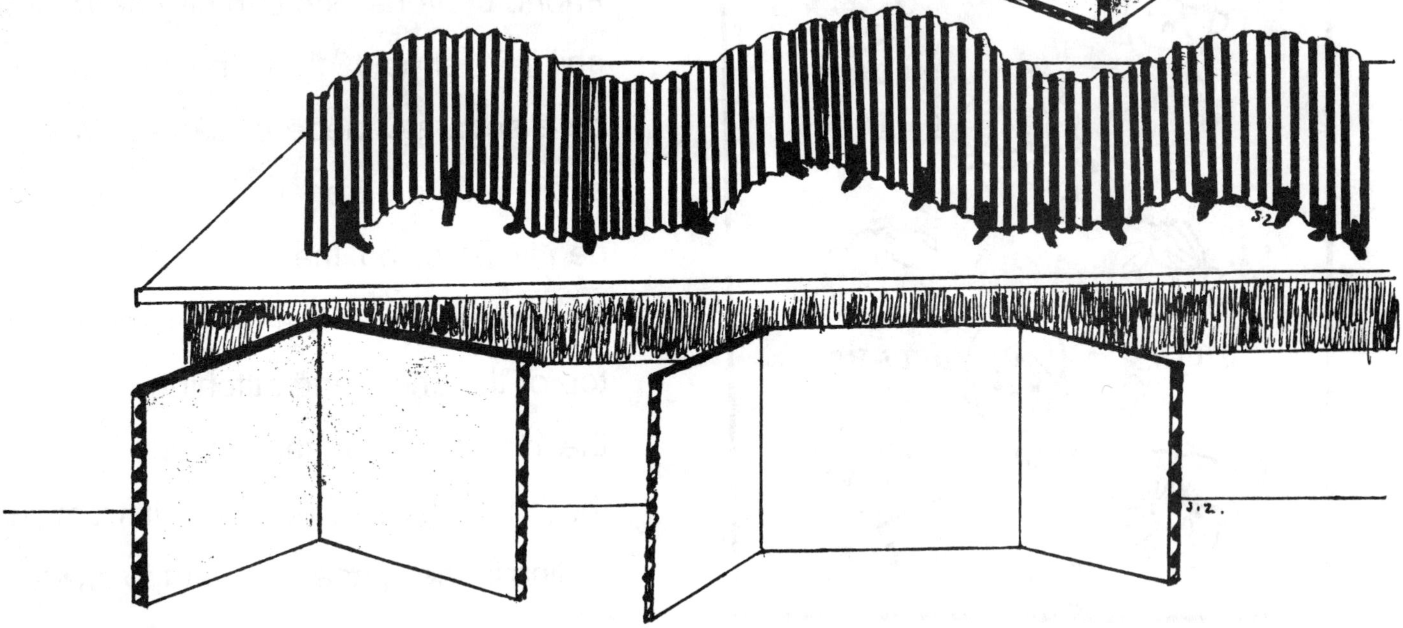

A long slab of corrugated paper will create working areas when placed on the top of a long table. Shape and tape it to the top of a table to form individual study areas. Decorations and task cards can be stapled or taped to both sides. Cardboard, scored and folded in the middle or in thirds, can be used to divide a surface into small areas.

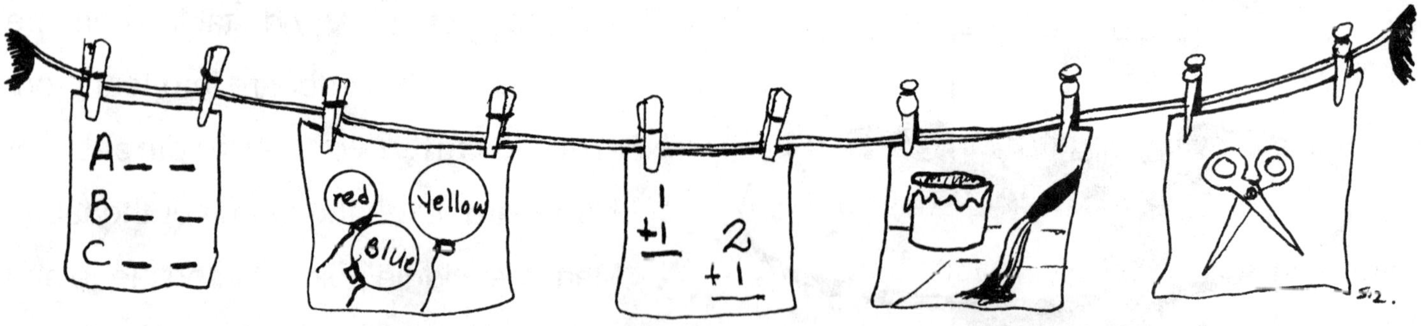


Hanging dividers can be used to create different learning sections for centers. A "clothesline" hanging across a window area, or from one side of the room to another, can be not only an attractive, but also a functional addition to your room. Make sure the wire is pulled taut. A wide variety of activities can be displayed with clothespins or paper clips. At student eye level, tasks can be hung in sequence, showing children which tasks to do. Hung lower, in the reach of small hands, children can manipulate the tasks.

Child-created dividers are colorful classroom additions. Children can decorate a large sheet, using felt pens. Fabric crayons also can be used. First, children should draw the decorations on a separate piece of paper. Then an adult with an iron can transfer it by gently pressing the colored side onto the sheet. Running a dowel across the top of the sheet and stitching the top of the material over the dowel will keep the sheet taut. Now, hang it from the ceiling in the space you want to divide.

Childrens' weaving also can be stitched or taped together to create a lovely hanging. A yarn stitchery done on burlap, by the class, can be hung similarly to the "sheet" hanging.

# STRUCTURING THE CLASSROOM

All children need structure. They need to know what the routine of the day will be. Too often centers have gained the reputation of "total openness," having no structure. Critics say children are free to do as they please and make their own learning decisions. In reality, though, any teacher who has ever attempted implementing centers in the classroom, realizes that the exact opposite is usually the case. In order for them to be successful, centers in the room require exacting organization and planning by the teacher. Only then will center time be a productive learning experience for all involved.

The prime ingredient for a successful center is for the teacher to feel in control and in charge of the situation at all times. Feeling comfortable about your classroom program will be conveyed readily to your perceptive students, as they watch your in-class reactions. That is why it is so important for you to realize there really is no one way for centers to be managed. They should be, instead, a product of you and of your experiences with kids. How often you would like centers in your classroom is again best determined by your judgment. Should your classroom be the "total center room" or the "monthly center experience"? That is your decision. Using centers in your room should certainly guarantee an interesting and hopefully rewarding teaching experience for you. Remember not only to "soak up" your students' enthusiastic center comments, but also to stop and analyze your mistakes. Like students, teachers can learn from their own mistakes. This realization will allow you to step back, evaluate a situation to find out what is wrong, what is right, and then plan for tomorrow.

# CAUTION !

Introducing too much, too soon, can lead only to confusion. It will be more productive, in the long run, to begin slowly and gradually introduce the center concept to your students. It is helpful to sit down and list all the concepts you will need to present to your students. In the excitement of setting up a center, one often loses sight of all the skills a child must have before he can use a center. Such basic concepts include the following:

# QUESTIONS TO ASK

1. Do my students know how to use all the materials at the center?
2. Do my students know where to put their work when they are finished?
3. Does the center need adult supervision?
4. Will all my students be able to do the tasks, or will certain students need special help? Which ones?
5. Should I limit the center to a certain number of students?
6. Should the center be used only at specified times?
7. How will I test to see whether the students are learning?
8. Are the students familiar with all the vocabulary words (if any) at the center?
9. Should students be allowed to work together at the center?
10. Are any math skills involved at the center that my students are unaware of?

As one can easily see, it is important to thoroughly analyze all aspects of a center before introducing it to the children. In this way, the center will be a much more pleasant experience for all concerned.

…g is an important concept … children to learn. Centers can be an excellent tool for teaching this concept. Having to make a decision will happen repeatedly as a child works at the center. "Which center will I work at today?" "Which task on my contract should I do today?" These are only a few of the decisions a child will need to make.

## DECISIONS.... DECISIONS!

It is important to remember, though, that decision making is a LEARNED concept. We must help children learn how to make decisions before they will be able to make valid ones. Initially, students should not be faced with too many choices. This can be done simply. Ask each student which center he would like to choose for the day, writing or math. Later, a child can be presented with three, four, or five choices. It is helpful sometimes to keep a record of which centers children choose for their first work place of the day. You will not only see which centers are most popular, but also the specific interests of each student. The choice a child makes may indicate that some students choose the same center each day. Do they need some direction from you?

| CENTERS for WEEK of *Sept. 20-28* | ART | DOLL HOUSE | MATH | BLOCKS | READING | SPELLING | WRITING | DINOSAURS | COOKING | |
|---|---|---|---|---|---|---|---|---|---|---|
| MARY | | ‖ | ‖ | \| | \|\|\| | ‖ | | \| | \| | never does art |
| SUSAN | 卌 | \| | | \| | \|\|\| | \| | | \| | | needs to change! |
| BILLY | \| | | \| | \| | 卌 | ‖ | \|\|\| | \|\|\|\| | | loves reading! |
| RICKY | \| | \| | \|\|\| | \| | ‖ | \| | \| | \|\|\| | \| | |

## NEW ITEMS

A new item in a center, such as a game involving many rules, may be introduced best at a totally separate time than when the center is introduced. Playing the game with a few students after recess, or explaining to a group during a class meeting, will allow more time for full understanding.

## TEACHER'S ROLE

Teachers play a large key role in creating the learning atmosphere. Centers may contain many manipulative materials and games that children often attribute to "playtime." Learning should be fun, but emphasize to the children it is "work time." By calling games "work tasks," and by asking children at which "work center" they would like to work, you are creating the classroom atmosphere.

## NOISE !

The noise level in your room is again up to your discretion. As children move around the room and work with each other, the noise level may increase. Stop! Listen! Is the noise busy and productive. If not, it may be time to turn out the lights and ask the children, "What's wrong with the room?" This technique, used a few times, will help remind the children what work standards and atmosphere you require. Also remember to stop and analyze your personal noise level. Has it increased above the children's level? A helpful rule for both you and your class to follow is that you may talk, but only loud enough for the friend next to you to hear you.

...games and tasks can be confusing. At a new center, it is helpful to ...t some familiar tasks, as well as a few new ones. The familiar activities will provide security to the children. The new task will be a challenge.

All of us like to know we have done a good job, especially children! If you see a child working particularly hard at a task, lending a hand to a friend, or cleaning up the center nicely, why not let the child (and the class) know about it? Jot down all your happy observations as you see them. After center time, have a special class meeting to share your observations. A handshake, special wink, sticker, or construction paper badge can be the reward. Your reward will be the smiles of honored classmates. Be sure to let all classmates know exactly why the award was given. Sit back and watch during the next center time. You will probably see others in your class working for special recognition.

## EVALUATION TIME

Just as it is useful to have a "pre-center talking time," it is also useful to have an "after-center talking time." This will provide an opportunity for children to discuss discoveries and problems. You may wish to ask:

* What did you learn?
* What was your favorite center?
* How did you work today?
* Any questions or problems?
* How can we improve center time tomorrow?
* Was anybody a special helper to a friend? How?
* Were there any centers you did not enjoy in the room? Why?

# THE DAY

Learning centers provide one alternative to the classroom structure. scheduling of the centers is a matter of teacher preference. Some teachers may choose to incorporate only weekly enrichment centers in their classrooms. Other teachers may choose to develop a total center approach. It is up to you! There are also many other ways to organize and use learning centers. Here is a possible plan that you might wish to develop.

The class meets each day for a planning time. Each child looks at his planning card to determine where he will work first. He informs the teacher, who makes note of the choice. By the end of your specified planning period, each member of the class must have completed the number of centers set by the teacher. The time duration of the center period, and how often students change centers, is a matter of teacher preference.

| CENTERS | MON. | TUE. | WED. | THURS | F |
|---|---|---|---|---|---|
| BOOK REPORT | Tom(T) | Pete Sue | Fred Pete* | Eric Pete | |
| SORTING | Chris Pete | Bob* Keith | Ted(T) Bob(T) Sue(T) | TOM | |
| PLANTS | Kris Chris | Kelly Ryan | Mark Sue | Robby Keith | |
| SPELLING | Kelly Mark | Bryan Kelly | Kelly Mark | Sue Carol* | |
| GRAPHS | Bob Fred | Chris(T) Carol(T) | Nan Chris | Carol Sue | |
| LISTENING | Jeb | | TIM | Bobby | |

TEACHER'S PLANS

## TEACHER'S PLANS

The teacher can have a weekly plan listing all the centers. As each child chooses a work area, the teacher notes the day and time on the plan sheet. At a glance, the teacher can see where each child has been and should be. Special notations can be made on the plan sheet, denoting special needs and assignments for specific children.

# ROBIN

"Round Robin" is another method of center structure that some teachers may wish to incorporate in the classroom. In this approach, the teacher divides the students into several groups. Each group works at the same center for a designated time period. The teacher may rotate the groups to a new center as often as she chooses. The following schedule is an example of how to arrange for groups to rotate twice each day.

| DATE | CENTER | I | II | III | IV | V | VI |
|---|---|---|---|---|---|---|---|
| Oct. 10 | 1st. | 1 | 2 | 3 | 4 | 5 | 6 |
| Oct. 10 | 2nd. | 6 | 1 | 2 | 3 | 4 | 5 |
| Oct. 13 | 1st. | 5 | 6 | 1 | 2 | 3 | 4 |
| Oct. 13 | 2nd. | 4 | 5 | 6 | 1 | 2 | 3 |
| Oct. 15 | 1st. | 3 | 4 | 5 | 6 | 1 | 2 |
| Oct. 15 | 2nd. | 2 | 3 | 4 | 5 | 6 | 1 |

| 1 | 2 | 3 | 4 | 5 | 6 |
|---|---|---|---|---|---|
| Larry | Peter | Frank | Jack | Jim | Mark |
| Mark | Joyce | Susie | Kate | Barbara | Tom |
| Tina | Peggy | Denise | Maxine | Tyler | Pam |
| Bob | Keith | Craig | Greg | Courtney | Steve |
| Sue | Cindy | Nancy | Jean | Chris | Kate |

For quick reference, post the students' names in their groups, somewhere visible to all in the room. A leader for each group can be appointed on a rotational basis. The leader is to be in charge of supplies and turning in completed work. Each group can be designated by a specific color. Students' names can appear on that color of construction paper on the bulletin board.

# INDIVIDUAL PLANNING

Each child should have a set of daily plans designed to meet his needs. Plans may be made only by the teacher or jointly with the child.

Each child's individual plan is kept in a plan folder for each week. This may be the complete plan or a supplement to a center contract.

| Date | Objective | Materials | Evaluation | Complete |
|---|---|---|---|---|
| 4/2 | Phoenics "ar" | Workbook p.40 | Mastered | X |
| 4/2 | Multip "5's" | X Box | Reinforce needed | — |
| 4/3 | Reading | choose 1 book | Good | X |
| 4/3 | Magnets | Ind. Project | Do again | — |
| 4/4 | Self-Awareness | Sound Center | | |

On Going Student Prescription Record ℞

NAME Billy T.

| TESTS | GOALS | METHODS/MATERIALS | EVALUATION |
|---|---|---|---|
| VADS | Improve Auditory Memory patterns | 1. Buzz boards<br>2. Aud. memory tapes<br>3. Frostig book Level II | 5 digit |
| Frostig | Develop Visual Motor Ability | Frostig Workbook Level II | retest |
| Gray Oral | Improve reading comp. from 3.2 to 4.0 | SRA Skill Builders<br>Basic Series Book 3.6<br>Cross Tutor | 5/2 = 3.4<br>6/8 = 3.8<br>reinforce |

An on-going "Student Prescription Record" will help the teacher continually to assess individual students' needs. This record will become a basis to develop additional plans, and can be used as an evaluation tool.

# ALL ABOARD! FOR ENRICHMENT & FREE TIME

The "ticket contract" is one way to set up an enrichment center. Each child is given a ticket to a special center in the room. (Tickets also may designate "free time" centers, to be used when children complete their work). Tickets are stored in a convenient place at the center. Each time the child works at the center, he/she is to punch the ticket on a dot. When all the dots have been punched, the child must give the ticket to the teacher, who will give him/her a new one. This gives you a good indication of who has been working at the center.

# WHERE IS EVERYBODY!!!?

A large chart is a convenient way to see where each child is working. It may be teacher controlled or child/teacher controlled. Students can move their name tags as they move from center to center.

Younger children will need pictures to help them. The chart alone is made from denim and has tape to divide areas. Pictures are made from real objects, which are glued or tied to the material. Childrens' names are added by writing them on clothespins which are clipped to the center they choose.

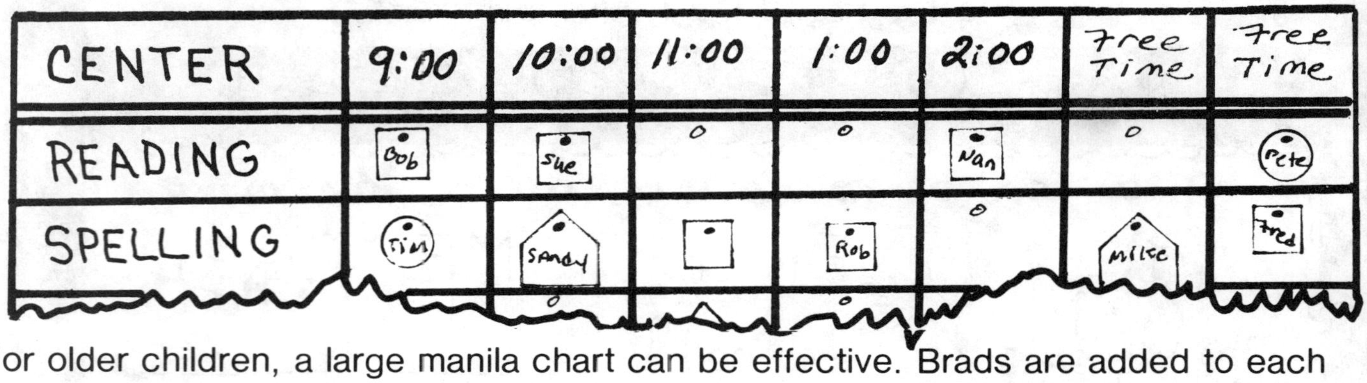


For older children, a large manila chart can be effective. Brads are added to each section. Name tags are made by punching a hole in the top to slip over the brad. Name tags cut into geometric shapes can denote a group. The group leader's name can be printed on the tag, set in a box showing the work task. This method also can be used for individuals.

# THE POCKET CHART

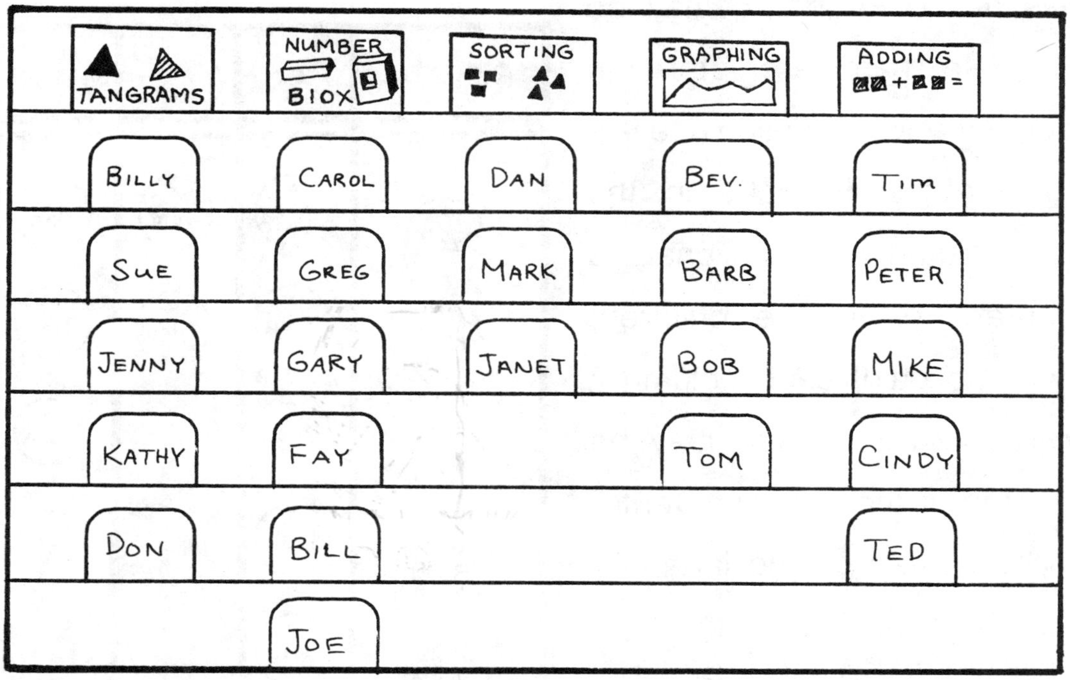


The "Pocket Chart Holder" can serve as an ideal center indicator. Center's areas and names can be removed and changed easily. This chart can be made from a vinyl window shade or a piece of oilcloth. There is no need to worry about who is where.

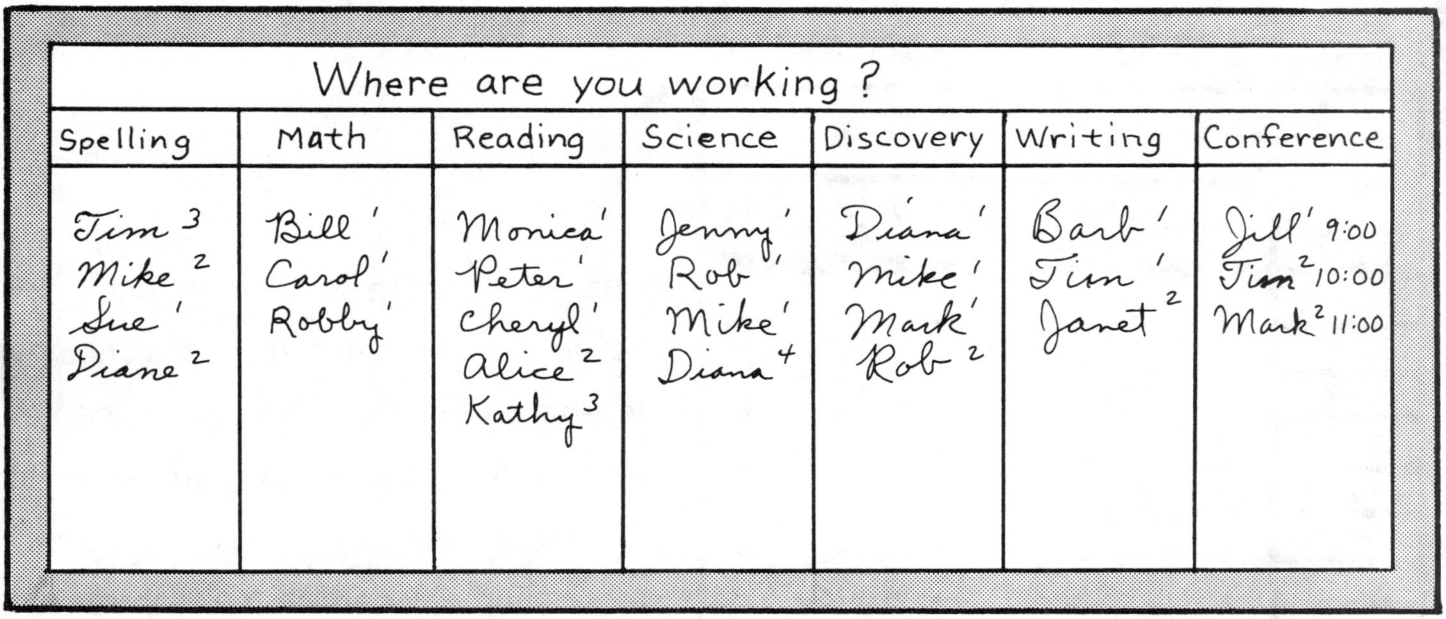


A chalkboard also can serve as a working index. Center topics can be changed easily. Children may write names each time they change centers. A number placed after students' names donates the students' working order.

# THE PEGBOARD CHART

The pegboard chart is a versatile chart for the classroom. Pegboard may be purchased at a hardware store in various sizes. One way you can use it is by placing purchased hooks in the holes. Each column may designate a different center. For younger children, you may wish to paint each column a different color. Masking tape may be taped to the top of the column. Center names can be written on the tape and easily removed by pulling off the tape when a center is to change. Circular tags also may be purchased. Write the name of each child on a tag. These then are hung in the appropriate center column.

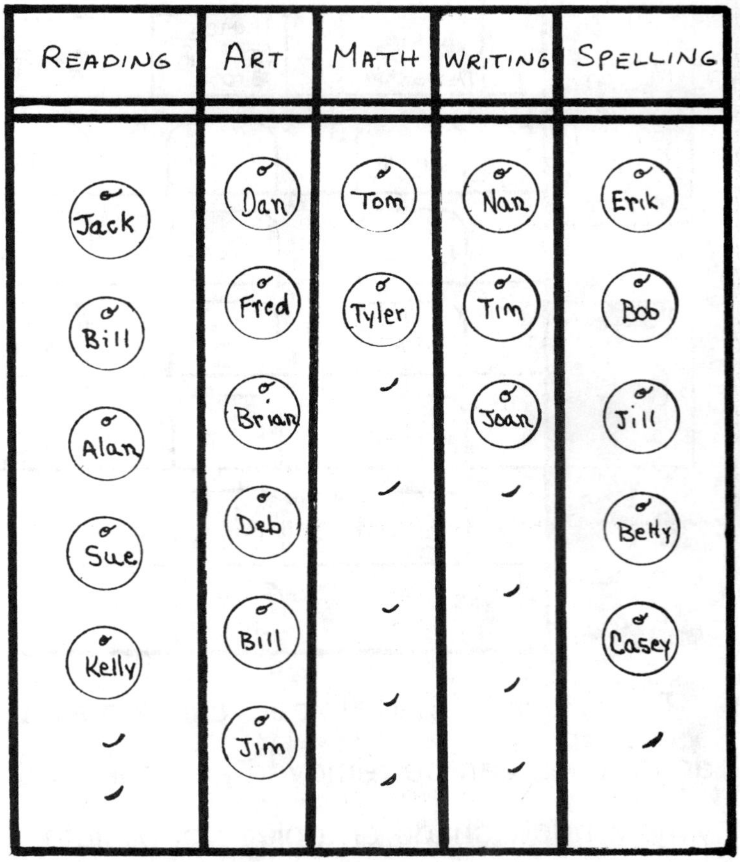


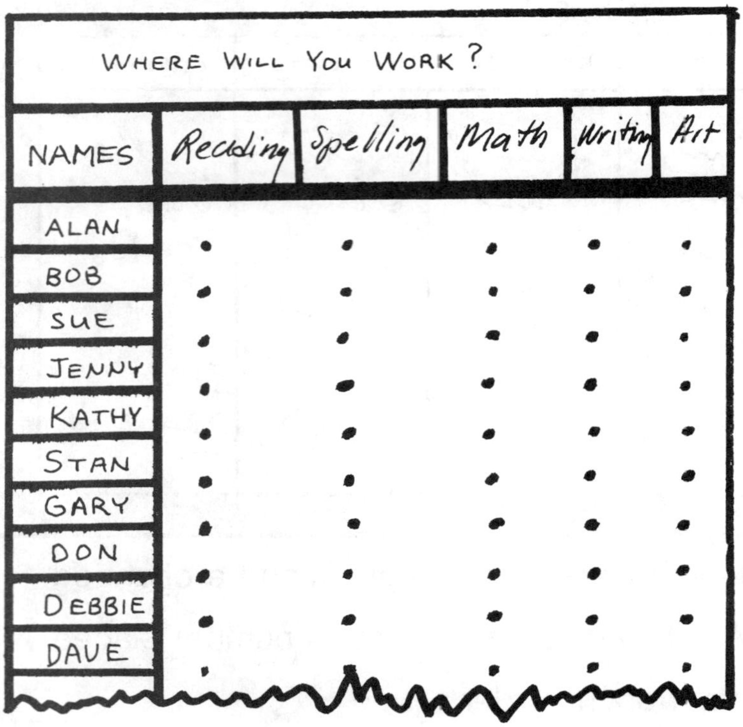


The pegboard also can be made by listing the children's names along the left-hand column and each center across the top. Pegs purchased in hardware stores, or teacher-supply stores, are placed in the appropriate holes by the children.

# COLOR CODING

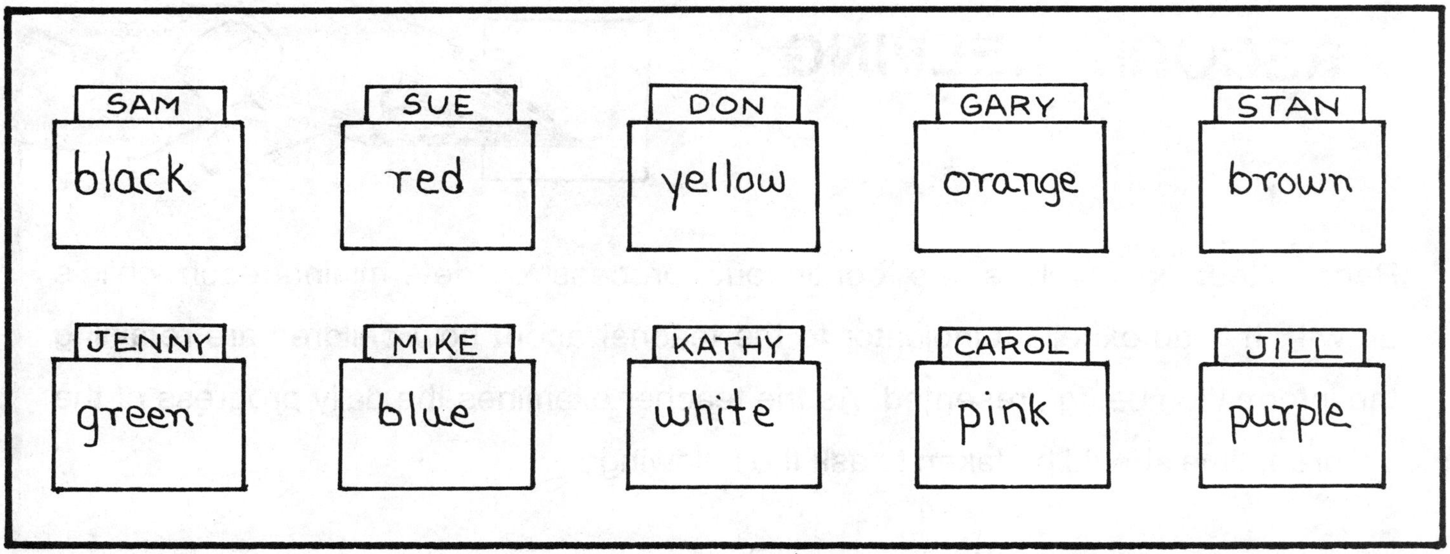


Color Coding the center index is an easy method for younger children to understand. A large chart is placed in the room. Library pockets are glued onto it. The names of the colors are printed on the pockets in the ink color matching the color word. The names of children who are to work in the center are written on cards and placed in the pockets.

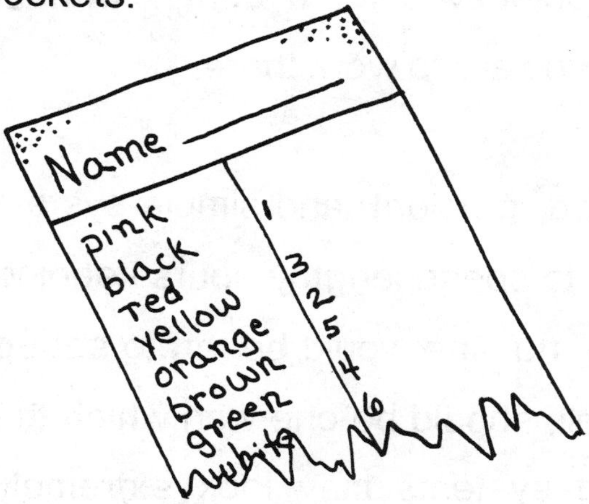


The corresponding centers around the room are marked with a round colored piece of construction paper. Again, the color word is printed on it. Ned would know exactly where he is to begin working.

A color coded contract for each child also may be used. A child may check where he is to be by looking at the order of the color words representing the centers. The teacher also may check at which centers the child should work. Write numbers to show the order in which work should be done.

# RECORD KEEPING

Record-keeping involves the continuous process of determining each child's growth. It is an excellent indicator to the teacher about how children are retaining the information being presented. As the teacher examines the daily progress of the children, time should be taken to ask the following:

....Do I need to reinforce the concept?
....Am I using the child's learning strengths?
....Am I challenging my students?
....Is the work on the child's level?
....Did I assess the task properly?
....How can I present the task again so the student will better understand it?

Record-keeping will become an integral part of any learning center program. It will be almost impossible for a teacher to develop objectives for a center without knowing the ability and knowledge of the students who are to work there.

The record-keeping system should be an organized, efficient, and simple system for the teacher. No teacher has the time or energy to spend lengthy hours keeping voluminous records on each child. If a teacher did, no time would be left to set up the centers. The record-keeping system, most of all, should be one with which the teacher feels comfortable. Many record-keeping systems may look extremely effective, but do not work, once in operation. Adapt the system to meet your needs. Find a simple, concise system that works for you and stick with it!

# HINTS

*If you plan to use the desks in your room as part of your centers, you will need a place for each child to keep his work. Ice cream cartons or plastic laundry bins make excellent storage containers. Students can easily carry them from place to place.

*A permanent place for children to turn in their work is a must! This can be a covered shirt box bottom. Always keep it in the same place.

*Remember contracts are excellent record-keeping devices. Specific performance behaviors can be written on the back of the contracts. The contract then can go into the child's permanent record folder, and a certificate showing completion of the contract can be sent home.

*Show capable children how to keep their own daily progress in a journal. The journal should be turned in each day, so you can make comments, suggestions, and assignments. Guidelines to writing the journals should be established and followed.

*Provide each child with a permanent manila folder. All skill sheets, old contracts, and observation sheets will go in the child's own folder. Only you and he/she may look inside. Keep all folders in an accessible record box.

## "THE CLIPBOARD"

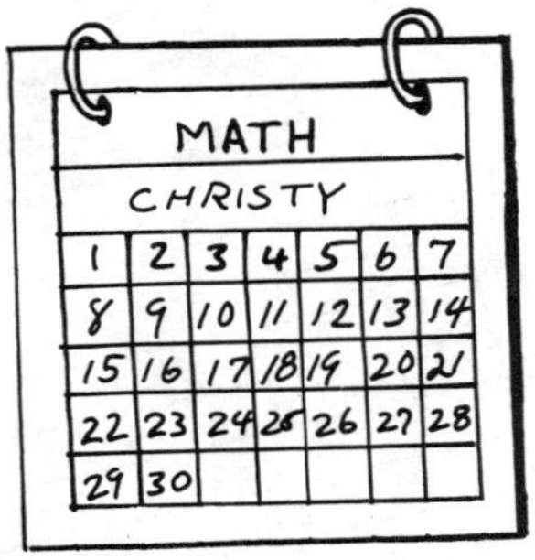


As the number of centers in your room increases, easy and efficient record-keeping systems become even more necessary. "The Clipboard" is an organizational record-keeping system that helps each child stay organized.

For each child, cut a thick piece of cardboard 9½" × 12". At the top of the clipboard, punch two holes about 1½" down from the top side. Each contract, that a child is currently working on, is punched in a similar manner. Attach the contracts and any accompanying performance skill sheets to the clipboard with metal rings. For children who need extra help in organizing themselves, put the contracts on the clipboard in the order you would like them to be done. Children may then flip each contract over as each task is finished, and begin work on the next assignment. To help remind children how many tasks you would like them to do on each contract, write the number in the top hand corner of the contract and circle it.

As a student's contracts increase in number, it is helpful for them to be color coded. A writing-center contract may be run off on pink construction paper. A corresponding pink circle can be pinned on the writing center area in the room. Math contracts may be blue; spelling contracts may be yellow.

To help you to see work assignments clearly, a daily or weekly work record for each child may be included on the front of their clipboard. You or the child should write down the task numbers to be completed on each contract. It is helpful if you and an aide begin the recording process for awhile. It will help children to work in sequence, if you desire, and you also will be able to tell quickly if a child has marked the wrong task and how much work has been completed. Seeing your system of recording will also give the child confidence to do his/her own record keeping.

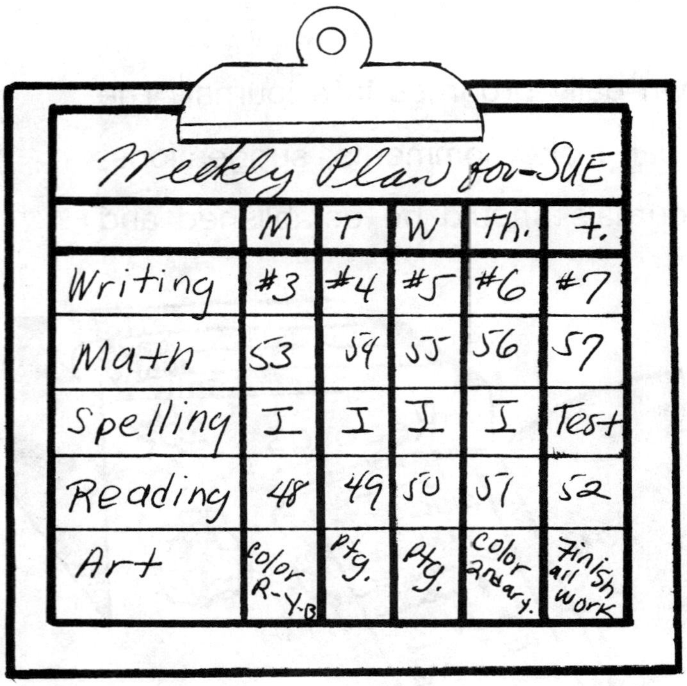

CONTRACTS

# CONTRACTS

Contracts are a very important part of any individualized, learning-center program. They are a record-keeping system not only for the teacher, but also for the child. They are effective not only for learning centers work, but also for individualizing workbook pages, task cards, and materials. On the back of the contract, note any special observations that will help to evaluate each child's progress more fully.

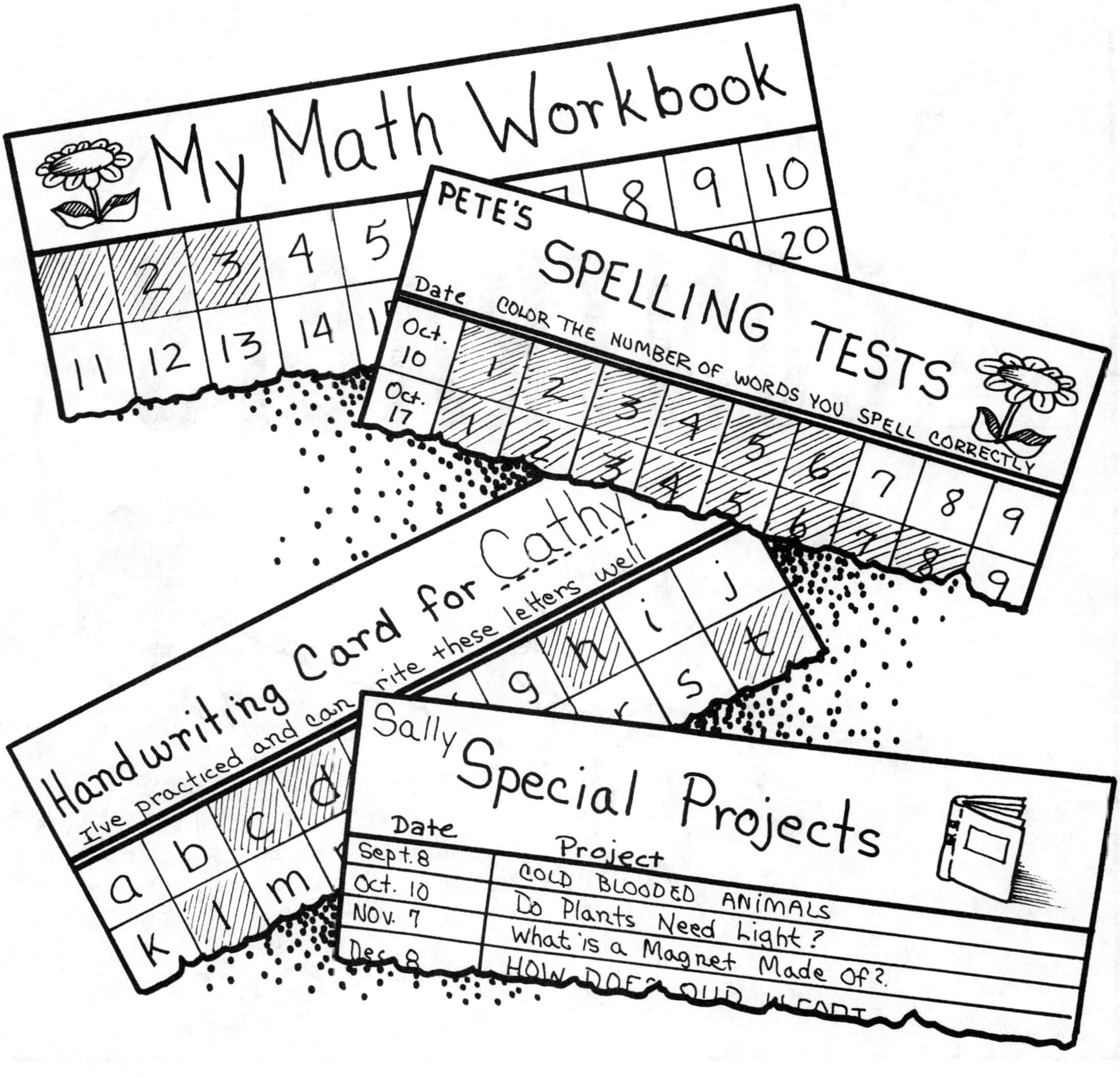

# CONTRACTS. . .CONTRACTS. . .CONTRACTS. .

There are numerous types of contracts that work effectively in learning centers.

| | | MY WORK |
|---|---|---|
| | black | LISTENING |
| | brown | TRACKING |
| 4 | green | CLOSURE |
| 3 | blue | SEQUENCE |
| | red | FINE MOTOR |
| 2 | white | SORTING |
| | orange | cat mat SOUND BLEND |
| 1 | purple | ADDING |
| 5 | yellow | READING |
| | gold | DISCRIMINATION |
| 6 | violet | BALANCE |
| | | |
| | | |

| MY WEEK | | |
|---|---|---|
| ACTIVITIES | MATERIALS | DATE |
| PAINTING | | |
| WRITING | | |
| SCIENCE | | |
| GRAPHING | | |
| PATTERN | | |
| LISTENING | | |
| SORTING | | |
| COOKING | | |

The teacher or student may choose the order in which the centers and center tasks are to be completed. Color code contracts to correspond to learning center areas, or identify contract and center with a corresponding symbol.

Centers in the room can be numbered. Each child has a contract with numbers that correspond to each center in the room. When a student completes a center, he then marks off the number on his contract.

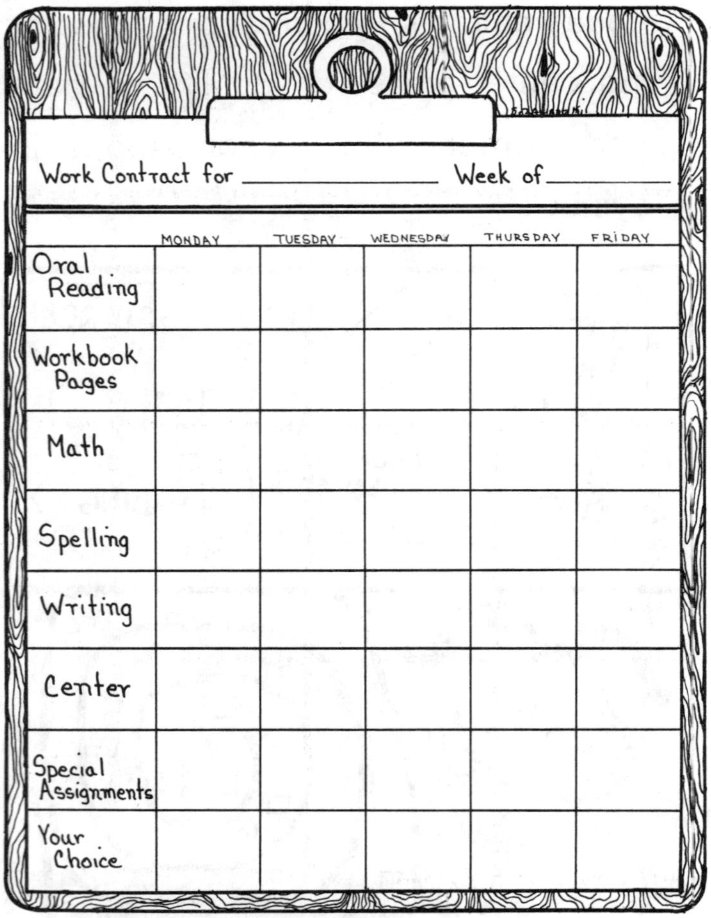


On this page are three samples of contracts that could be used with students. Contracts for primary children should remain relatively simple. Throughout the book you will find several more samples.

# WEEKLY CONTRACT

A nonreading child can "read" his daily schedule through pictures. He/she may choose which centers he/she will work at each day, by coloring in the box by the picture. Specific tasks can be written by the teacher. A more structured program can be created by the teacher, who writes numbers by the centers. These clue the child to the sequence he will work that day. Each day the teacher can check work.

| Jimmy 6/7 | MONDAY | TUESDAY | WEDNESDAY | THURSDAY | FRIDAY |
|---|---|---|---|---|---|
| Spelling | 2 | Take Spelling Test | | Careful! | |
| Blocks | 1 | | "REDO" Area card | | FINISHED CONTRACT ☺ |
| Science | 4 | | | * Have you finished? | |
| Painting | 5 | I liked your story - REMEMBER CAPITAL LETTERS | | | |
| Reading | 3 | Read pages 50-51-52 | | Nice Reading | |
| Music | 6 | | Start your instrument | | |
| Teacher | Conference 9:00 | | Get new book for report. | | |

# HELPING CHILDREN SEE THEIR PROGRESS

All of us like to know we are improving when we are working hard at a task. Children are no different. Keeping track of children's progress will not only be beneficial to your students' self-images, but also will be very handy as record-keeping devices.

Each child also should play a role in charting his own progress. At the beginning of the year, give each child a manila folder with his/her name on the top. These folders can be kept in a special location, and can be marked "Our Best Work." As the year progresses, have children fill their folder with samples of their best work. Be sure to date each sample in the top corner.

Work samples also can be kept in a large work-folder envelope made by each child. Fold over a sturdy piece of paper and punch holes along two sides of the folder. Children can lace around three sides of the folder with colorful yarn. Paintings, dictated stories, and other samples of special work can be included.

**Fill in the faces to show YOU at center time.**

Good!

Okay!

Can do better!

1. I worked like this: 

2. I cleaned up like this: 

3. I was a helper like this: 

4. The center made me feel like this: 

5. I got this much work done: 

**NAME** ____________________ **CENTER** ____________________

This evaluation can be completed at the end of each center time by each child. It can be read outloud together for nonreaders. Forms for each child can be kept together in a special "Center Notebook." This will allow you to easily see changes in individual childrens' attitudes.

# WOW AWARD!

This special award is

to certify that ________________

has completed the ______________

________________ contract.

Date ____________________

Signed __________________

## SPECIAL PROJECT CONTRACT

The subject I want to learn more about

______________________________________

I want to find out.....

______________________________________

I will show what I learned by....

______________________________________

Special materials I will need....

______________________________________

I will start my project on ____________
I expect to finish my work by __________

________________ Student ________________ Teacher

## SPECIAL REPORT

by ________________________

Subject ____________________

**Book Title** **Author**

________________ ________________

________________ ________________

What interesting things did you learn about this subject?

______________________________________

Draw a picture of your favorite part.

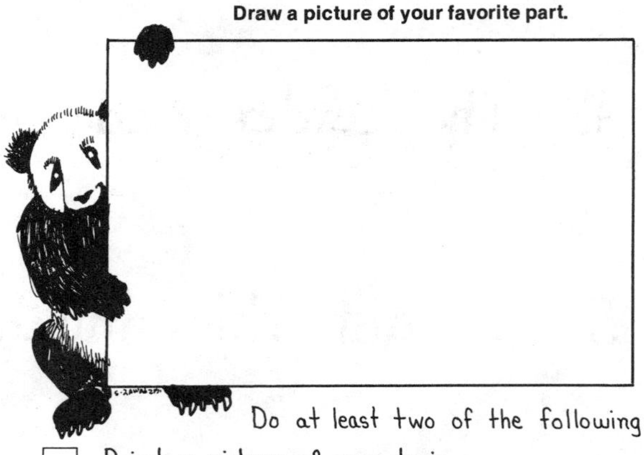

Do at least two of the following:

- ☐ Paint a picture of your topic.
- ☐ Write a guessing riddle about your subject.
- ☐ Share your report with a friend.
- ☐ Make a diorama.
- ☐ Find another book about your topic.
- ☐ Make a mobile about your topic.
- ☐ List some new words that you learned.

______________________________________

# RECORDING PROGRESS

It is important for teachers to be able to measure how much children have learned at a center. By pre-testing the children's knowledge about the topic, the teacher will be able to develop appropriate tasks at a center. Testing the children at the end of the unit, will allow the teacher to determine how much knowledge was gained. There are many different methods of measuring a child's growth. These methods need not be just tests involving the "multiple choice" and "true/false" variety. Tests are actually made to determine how much the teacher has grown and learned about the students.

Pre-testing children to see how much knowledge they have about a particular concept, could be as easy as asking each child to write as much as they know about the topic. Reading over the pages will give you information, not only about the extent of knowledge a child has about the topic, but also a general idea of the child's strengths and weaknesses concerning the topic. At the end of a unit, children can be post-tested in the same manner.

Concepts can also be tested verbally by tape recording. Have each child bring a cassette tape to school. Be sure his name is on it. Periodically, children can record their oral reading progress by recording their best reading passage. Poetry, auditory memory, and verbal expression can also be tested.

## Other examples of pre and post tests include:

MATCHING

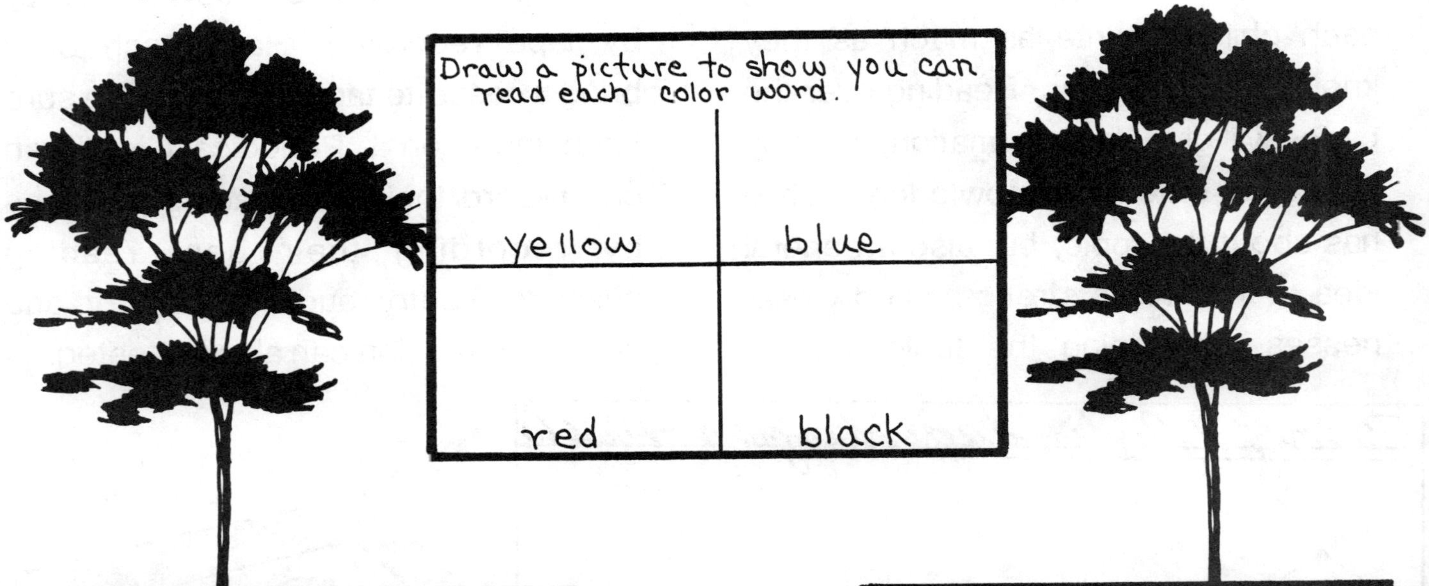


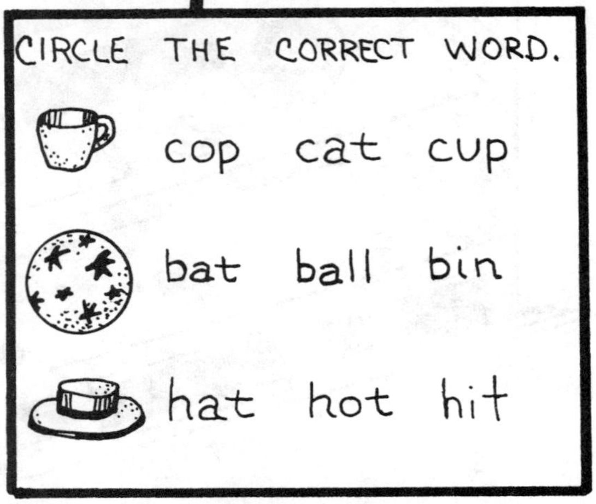


MULTIPLE CHOICE

TRUE-FALSE

# OBSERVATION SHEET

Duplicate a chart with each child's name on it. Keep the chart handy, within arm's reach. Throughout the day, make note of any academic/behavior observations that would be helpful when planning next week's Student Programs.

| NAME Tim | OBSERVATION SHEET | DATE 11/5 |
|---|---|---|
| TYLER | Help again at motor station. | |
| DANNY | Send spelling envelope home. Show how to use listening post. | |
| ALAN | Works well with Danny. MATH — work on AREA | |
| CHRIS | ✓ progress in leaf center. send home work packet. | |
| DEBBIE | | |
| COURTNEY | TAKES TIME TO HELP OTHERS b/d reversal | |
| ANN | assign special topic — let her choose | |
| COLLEEN | set up time with cross-tutor call mother — crying | |
| TRACY | ready for "AR" combination | |
| BRIAN | check READING FOLDER | |
| ERIK | ready for "AR" combo. — pair with Tracy help Danny with spelling. | |
| BOB | Birthday Fri. difficulty discriminating i/e sounds | |
| | | |
| | | |

## INVENTORY

TOPIC

| NAME | | | | | | | | | |
|---|---|---|---|---|---|---|---|---|---|
| | | | | | | | | | |
| | | | | | | | | | |
| | | | | | | | | | |
| | | | | | | | | | |
| | | | | | | | | | |
| | | | | | | | | | |
| | | | | | | | | | |
| | | | | | | | | | |
| | | | | | | | | | |
| | | | | | | | | | |
| | | | | | | | | | |
| | | | | | | | | | |
| | | | | | | | | | |
| | | | | | | | | | |
| | | | | | | | | | |

## STUDENT'S CENTER PERFORMANCE SCALE

Student ____________________ Date __________

| Center Performances | DOES NOT APPLY | NEEDS TO IMPROVE | SATIS-FACTORY | DOING WELL |
|---|---|---|---|---|
| ① Makes effective use of center time. | | | | |
| ② Completes required assignments. | | | | |
| ③ Works well independently. | | | | |
| ④ Works well in small groups. | | | | |
| ⑤ Understands directions ORAL WRITTEN | | | | |
| ⑥ Makes effective use of materials. | | | | |
| ⑦ Student makes use of all centers. | | | | |
| ⑧ Others | | | | |

RECOMMENDATIONS:

NAME DATE

## WEEKLY STUDENT PRESCRIPTION SHEET

| | | | | | | | | | | | | |
|---|---|---|---|---|---|---|---|---|---|---|---|---|
| COMPLETION | | | | | | | | | | | | |
| EVALUATION PERFORMANCE | | | | | | | | | | | | |
| MATERIALS/TECHNIQUES | | | | | | | | | | | | |
| EDUC. OBJECTIVE | | | | | | | | | | | | |
| DATE | | | | | | | | | | | | |

## ONGOING STUDENT PRESCRIPTION RECORD

NAME

BIRTHDATE

| | |
|---|---|
| TESTS | |
| EDUC. GOALS/OBJ. | |
| METHODS—MATERIALS—TECHNIQUES | |
| EVALUATION | |

# INFORMING PARENTS ABOUT CENTERS

Nothing will be reinforcing to your attitude, and your classroom program, as having the students' parents tell you that their children love school. Having center activities in your room almost guarantees positive comments to occur. As your class discovers the joy of actively taking part in their own learning, their excitement will be transmitted to their parents through dinner time discussions about school.

Parents are, of course, primarily concerned with how much their child is learning in school. If parents have not had a chance to visit the classroom during school time, they often will base the amount of their child's learning by the number of completed work papers in Friday's folder. As teachers, we must help acquaint our students' parents to understand what goes on in the classroom each day. Parent support of the program will be reinforcing to everyone involved. Enthusiasm is certainly contagious. "Back-to-School Night," or any evening meeting, involving you and your students' parents, is a good time to explain your centers.

Be sure to mention how often children will be going to the centers and which concepts you hope to teach. Have plenty of examples handy, including a few current projects children are working on, as well as sample contracts. Once you show parents their children's contracts, and how they work, the parents will be much more aware of progress. It might even be fun to have parents spend a few minutes at a center and complete an activity or two from their child's contract! This would be a good time to mention that, because children are actively taking part in their learning and using actual objects to make their discoveries, not as many ditto papers may be coming home.

Throughout the year you will want to continue to inform parents about new centers and happenings in the room. A classroom newspaper, published weekly or monthly by the children, will not only help parents learn what their children are doing in school, but also will be a good learning experience for the children. Each edition can contain "Center News" and Class Happenings." Also be sure to include the best stories and pictures from class artists and authors. Articles can be printed by the children on ditto masters and duplicated by a cross-age tutor or parent aide.

Center journals written by each child about center work experiences also can be informative to parents. Journals can be sent home periodically, or as they are completed.

A "center scrapbook" filled with the children's descriptions of learning discoveries, and photographs of center activities is a fun way for a visitor to learn about your classroom.

Dear Parents,

Can you please help us? Frequently, there are things at home that you don't need anymore that could be used at school. The following is a list of things we could use in our classroom to help create our new learning centers. Please check items you can donate and return this form with your child tomorrow.

Thank you for your interest and cooperation!

Furniture to help create learning center areas in the classroom:

________rugs (any size) ________bookcases
________couch ________wooden crates
________screens (folding) ________rocking chairs
________book ends ________pillows

Materials that could be used in the centers:

________lumber, odds and ends (small please!)
________material: felt scraps, burlap, yardage scraps
________stitchery items: hammers, nails, saws
________magazines, calendars, catalogs
________yarn, buttons, rickrack, lace, sequins
________egg cartons ________clothespins
________minute timers ________tin cans, plastic containers
________children's books ________old records
________coloring books ________wallpaper books
________cooking utensils (mixing bowls, measuring cups, pans, pot holders).
________other: ______________________________________________
_______________________________________________________________

Signed ______________________________________

# PARENT AIDES

To help you manage your centers, you might like to have parent aides in your classroom. With the proper training, parent aides can be extremely beneficial to a learning center program. You will find you finally have the extra time you never had before to work with children who need your special help, as well as to do those extra projects you thought you would never get finished.

It is best to introduce the use of aides gradually to your classroom structure. It is helpful for everyones' peace-of-mind to first have aides that you feel comfortable with in your classroom. Be selective! If you do not feel a particular parent will be just right, ask the parent to please do special clerical home tasks such as correcting or making new dittos.

Parent aides will, of course, be the most effective for you if you clearly let them know what you want them to do. You might want to have an after-school training program to explain your classroom in detail. Parents will need to know where all the materials are located, how to operate special equipment, where they can pick up their assignments for the children, and any classroom standards you would like emphasized. Having a training program in advance, will help alleviate all the in-class questions that take up so much time.

Before eliciting parent help, sit down and make up a thorough list of all the possible ways you will need parents. By each item, list whether it is an "at-home" or "in-class" task, and the approximate number of hours per week you think you will need help. This list can be sent home with your students as a flyer, asking for parent aides. Once you know which tasks parents would like to do and for how long, you can begin having conferences and making assignments.

# CALLING ALL PARENTS!

Dear Parents,

Can you please help us? We're off to such a great start toward having an outstanding learning year. We have so many activities and projects planned. We could certainly use your help! Please check any of these items you would be willing to help with and send this form with your child, tomorrow. I will be in touch with you soon to let you know about your assignment.

____work in the classroom, in the learning centers, an hour (or more!) a week.

____correct math tests at home, when your child brings them home.

____at home, one time a week, correct papers from the reading kit.

____run off dittos at school.

____help at the stitchery center at school.

____help at the cooking center at school.

____help prepare art projects at school.

____help make dittos at home.

____help laminate materials at school.

____give a special presentation to the children on a subject we will be studying in school...(science experiments, poetry reading, show slides of a trip you have taken.)

____help at the carpentry center at school.

____help children in the classroom garden.

____listen to children read at school.

____provide transportation for field trips.

____make cookies for special occasions.

Signed ______________________________

The days that I could help are: ______________________________

______________________________

The times of day I could help are: ______________________________

______________________________

Parent's Signature ______________________________

# AIDES

Set aside a special place in the classroom for aides to check in each time they come to the room.

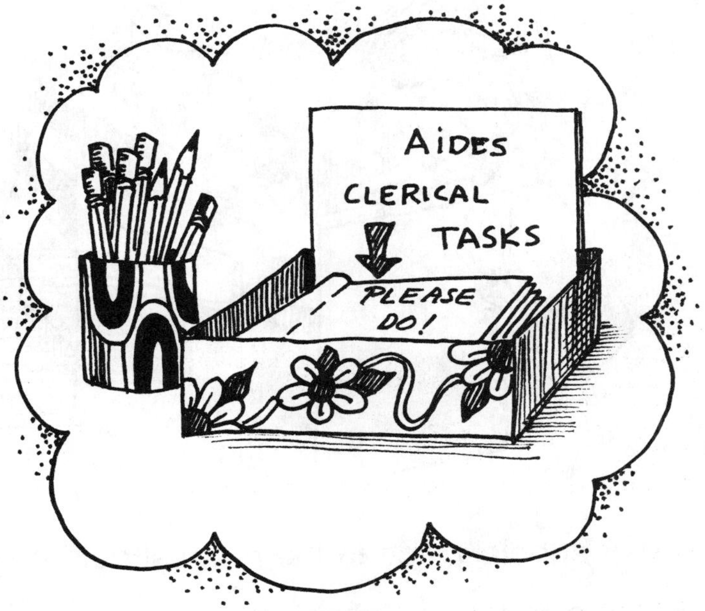


Aides will also need to know which tasks you would like them to do for the day. Clerical tasks, such as running off dittos, mending games, or laminating projects, can be put in a large box marked "Clerical Aides Tasks." Be sure to include all supplies needed to complete the task and a note providing any special instructions.

Instructional directions for aides working with children also need to be conveniently placed. You can plan their tasks ahead of time using an "aide instructional task sheet". List which aide you would like to work with which child. A brief description of the task could be as simple as "page 53, math book." You will want to know the positive/negative aspects of each work session. Aides may fill in their evaluation of the work sessions using the sheet titled "Aide's Evaluation." Aides may also wish to let you know such facts as: "Sarah had difficulty on this page," or "Assignment was very easy, Bill could do it on his own."

A class meeting, held before parent-aides begin to work in your room, may be advisable. Explain to your children who the parents are and why they will be working in the room. It may be helpful to go over class standards that you will expect when the helpers are in the room. Then enjoy the results!

# CROSS AGE TUTORS

A program which will provide extra help for classroom students, as well as helping your centers to move smoothly, is "Cross Age Tutors." These children come from another classroom, typically two to three grade levels ahead of the class, in which the tutoring is to occur. In order for the program to be efficient, organization is a must!

A special place in the room should be set aside as a "check-in" spot. At this spot, provide any materials the tutor may need to use with a student, an evaluation form for the tutor to fill in, and any specific notes you have for the student(s). Often you will not have enough time to tell the tutor everything you would like. Write it down! This will make things so much more official.

Sometime, you may wish to have an after-school training session for "Cross Age Tutors." This would be an in-class discussion on ways to help students, specific behavioral goals you are working towards and a chance to learn location of all the materials. It would also be a chance for the "Big Buddies" to ask questions about how to help their "Little Buddies."

# PORTABLE CENTERS!

Very often classroom centers are designed to foster the development of a specific academic skill. You will discover that not all the children in your room are ready at the same time for a specific center. The "portable center" is the answer to individualization, as well as to organization. The portable center remains intact with sequenced activities, games, worksheets, and contracts, and should be kept in a convenient place in the room until another child is ready to use it.

CONTRACT

ACTIVITY BOX

ACTIVITY ENVELOPE

Each task in a portable center should be numbered at the top right-hand corner for easy visibility and reference. Directions for the task should be placed on the outside of the envelope. Any material needed for the task should be placed inside.

# HOW TO MAKE PORTABLE CENTERS!

1. Any grocery store box wide enough to adequately hold your planned activities will work. Make sure it is long enough to hold a stationery store envelope (or whatever type you choose to use to store your activities). The box should also be trimmed enough to conveniently fit in the storage area you have designated.

2. Decorate your box colorfully. It is helpful if you choose an easily recognizable motif to place both on the outside of the box, on the contract, and on each activity holder. This will help the children to clean up quickly and return any loose items to the proper place. Motifs can include balloons, butterflies, inchworms, flowers, hearts, or frogs. See illustrations below. You may wish to cover the storage box with contact paper and place small pieces of the same paper on each activity folder.

3. Each activity should be clearly numbered in the top right-hand corner of the envelope. Additional material inside the envelope should also be numbered on both sides with corresponding numbers. For younger children, not quite familiar with number recognition, the corresponding number of dots can be included under the number. This also will help children to keep the activities sequenced.

4. A colorful contract can be made easily on a duplicating master and copies made on construction paper. Each child should have his/her own contract for purposes of record keeping. As the child completes an activity, he/she may color in the number on his/her contract that corresponds to the number of the completed activity.

5. Task cards for the center should be laminated or covered with clear contact paper for durability. This also will allow the children to write with a watercolor pen, their answers to the tasks directly on the cards. This will save the teacher much time, because worksheets will not need to be made. Answers can be erased with a damp sponge or cloth.

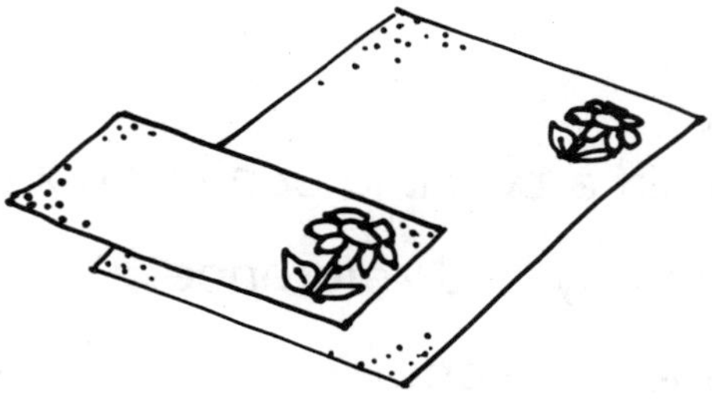

# INTRODUCTION OF BOXES

It is important to acquaint children thoroughly with the portable box centers before they begin the actual tasks. This way children can devote their work energies to the concept/skill and not to the mechanics of the box. It is very beneficial, first to introduce the class to a very easy box, designed primarily to provide practice. A Puzzle Box is an enjoyable way to begin.

# PUZZLE BOX:

Round up all the old puzzles in your classroom. Parents can be very helpful here, too. Remember, for easy storage, these activities should each fit inside the stationery envelope. Label each task envelope with a number. Make up a contract corresponding to the number of puzzles. Contracts can be stored in the front of the box. Colorfully label the box with pictures so that children can easily identify the box. Old puzzle pieces can be glued to the front and sides of the box.

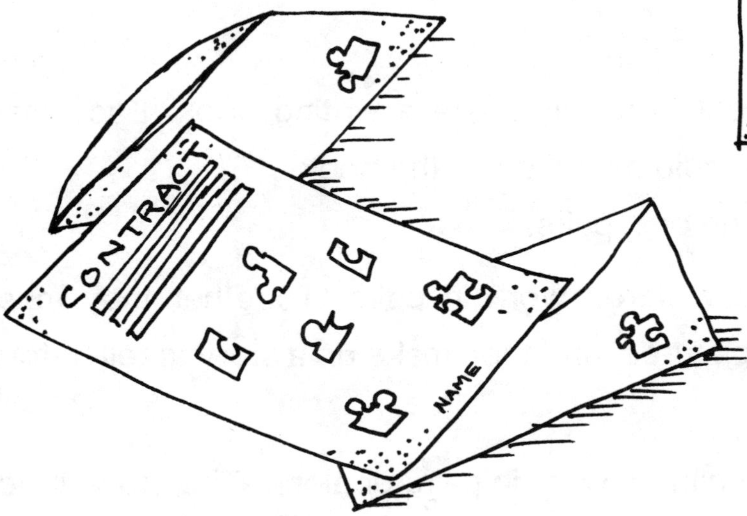


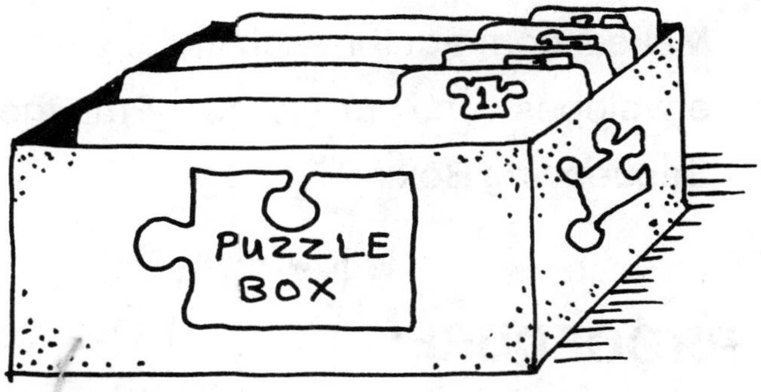


1. Be sure to identify the Activity Envelope by number.
2. Don't forget to number all task pieces that belong in each envelope.
3. Students color a puzzle piece as work is completed.

# SEQUENCING BOX

The Sequencing Portable Box Center is another enjoyable center that is also a good classroom introduction to portable centers. It will help develop sequencing and oral language skills.

**MATERIALS:**

You will need a series of sequence pictures depicting a theme. Old workbooks and the Sunday comics are excellent sources. Glue each set on tagboard, laminate, cut apart, and place inside an activity envelope.

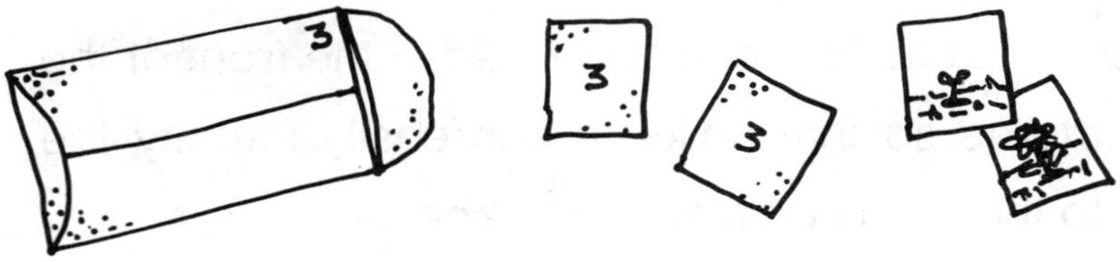

Label the back of each section with the same number appearing on the activity envelope.

Make a contract for each child. On the contract put the same amount of numbers as envelopes you prepared. Put the activity envelopes and contracts in the Sequencing Box.

**PROCEDURE:**

Older children may make a writing book. Each task story should be written in the book.

Children may complete each task alone or in pairs.

To increase verbal ability, have the children work in pairs. Together they must decide the correct sequence of the pictures, and then make up a story to tell before the task is checked complete.

To increase written ability, have the children work in pairs or alone. The story about the pictures is written down in a writing book for each child.

# "REMEMBERABLES"

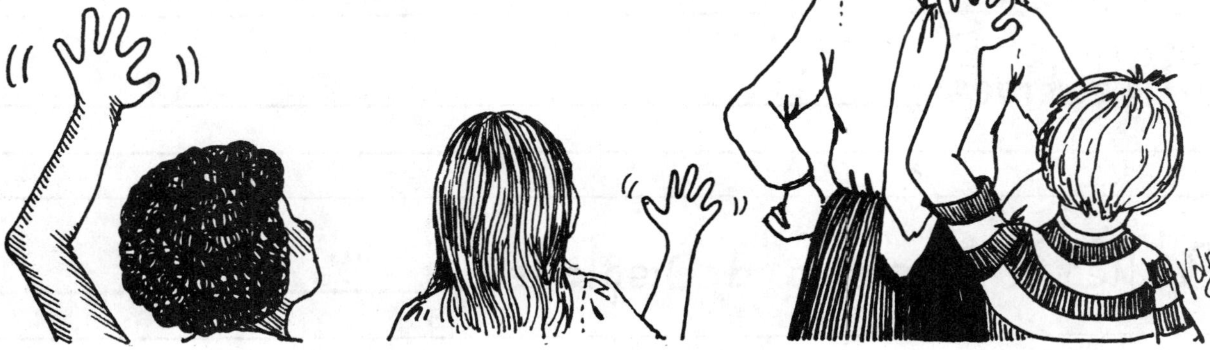

1. Introduce the class to the new center during a discussion time. Inform your students what the new center will help them learn. It is sometimes easier to introduce new centers on a day other than Monday, so concentration will be better.

2. Each child will be responsible for his/her own contract. Contracts should be kept in the front of the box. As the child completes a task, he/she raises his/her hand. The teacher then marks off the appropriate number on the student's contract. A good rule to establish is that students may NOT clean up a task until it has been "checked." To help develop verbal abilities of your children, have them explain to you what they did as well as showing you. The child may then color in the number of the completed task on his/her contract.

3. Cleaning up properly is a must! Demonstrate how to correctly clean up a task. Other children also can role play "clean up." Envelopes that have brads on them may be difficult to manipulate. Show children how to open and close the brad. Look around for all the task pieces. Sometimes it is helpful for children to work on a "place mat." A colored piece of construction paper kept at the working spot can serve as a place mat. All task pieces remain on the paper during work time. These rules should allow for efficient and easy "clean ups."

4. Tasks requiring written answers will need additional explanation. If your task cards are laminated, children can write directly on them with watercolor pens. A damp sponge will remove the writing. Watercolor pens, and sponges cut in one inch cubes, should be kept in a designated area in the room. Sponges and pens should be returned at the end of use.

# CENTER CHECKLIST

TOPIC ______________________________

Objectives ______________________________

______________________________

______________________________

Bulletin Board and Displays ______________

______________________________

______________________________

Visual Aids (films, charts, pictures, displays) ______

______________________________

______________________________

______________________________

______________________________

Library Books

______________

______________

______________

______________

______________

Poems, Songs, Records

______________

______________

______________

______________

______________

Materials needed (art)

______________

______________

______________

______________

______________

Worksheets/Learning Materials

______________

______________

______________

______________

______________

Special Equipment ______________________________

______________________________

______________________________

______________________________

______________________________

# Center Activities

**Math** ____________________

**Reading** ____________________

**Writing** ____________________

**Art** ____________________

**Additional** ____________________

Group activities (art, drama, stories, projects ...)

Special activities (field trips, guest speakers ....)

Supplies (from home)

REMEMBER!

# MINI CENTERS

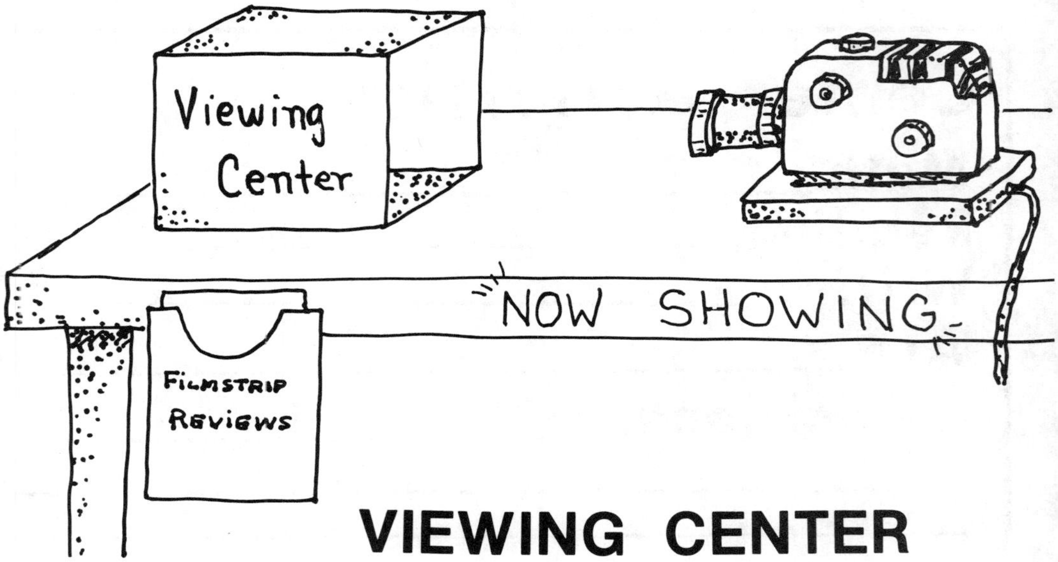


## VIEWING CENTER

The Viewing Center can be set up as a semi-permanent station in your room. This center can be used with many different contract topics. Numerous excellent filmstrips are available at county education offices and libraries. The filmstrips can be shown at a reading table near an electric outlet and projected into a grocery box. Paint or cover the box with black. Staple a white piece of paper on the inside bottom of the box. Turn the box on its side and provide ample Filmstrip Review worksheets. (See next page.) Your center is complete!

## PAINTING CENTER

A permanent paint center also will be a handy addition to your classroom. Easels are ideal but tables or shelf areas can be covered with newspapers and used. Keep a large jar of water in the sink for children to wash their brushes. Paint shirts can be brought from students' homes. Extra newspapers and plenty of paint paper should be kept handy. A clothesline, hung under a cupboard or shelf, provides a great drying line.

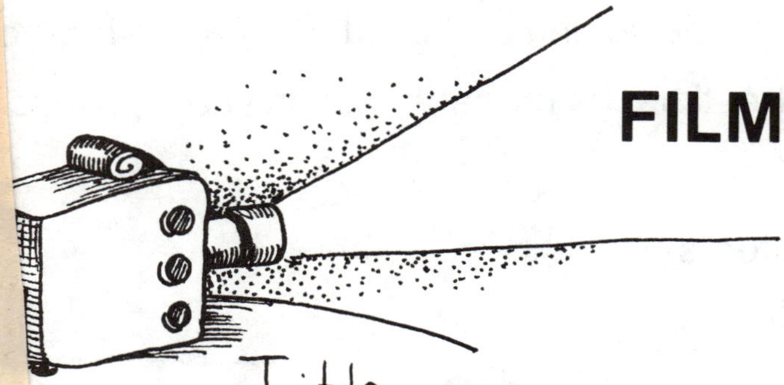

# FILMSTRIP REVIEW

Title ______________________________

Name of reviewer ______________________________

Name two new things you learned from the film.

Draw something you saw in the film.

# THE DAY OF RECKONING

After all your planning, re-planning, designing and building of a center, your "day of reckoning" will occur. It will be time to present the finished product, "THE CENTER", to your class.

A good time to present a new center is at a class meeting (large group). Having the class sit around the center display will acquaint them with all the materials involved. Many teachers prefer to begin new centers on a day other than Monday, since younger children often tend to be more excitable after a weekend. This also will allow you time to "set up" the day before, after the children have gone home. Allow a lot of time for questions and more questions.

It will be, of course, important for you to emphasize the care of the materials. Special equipment, such as a filmstrip projector, will need special demonstrations. If you have a particularly fragile item at the center, be sure to point it out. Once children realize how to care for equipment, they will be much more conscientious. Role-playing, how to use the center, and how to clean up the center by classmates, will be a fun and productive learning experience. Classmates can also role-play the wrong way, by using the center to see if other friends can catch their mistakes.

# A Center in Action

# DINOSAUR LAND

**Purpose:** To familiarize students with animals of the past and their habitats. To plot objects on a bar graph. To improve visual and auditory comprehension. To strengthen fine motor development.

# DINOSAURS

by ____________________

Look at the film-strip about dino-saurs. Do the filmstrip review worksheet.

Make a dinosaur shape book. Write a story about dinosaurs on scratch paper. Carefully copy it in the shape book. Illustrate your book.

READ Danny and the Dinosaur by Sid Hoff. Paint a picture of your favorite part.

My dinosaur is ____________________
Find information about your favorite dinosaur. Where did he live? What size was he? What did he eat?

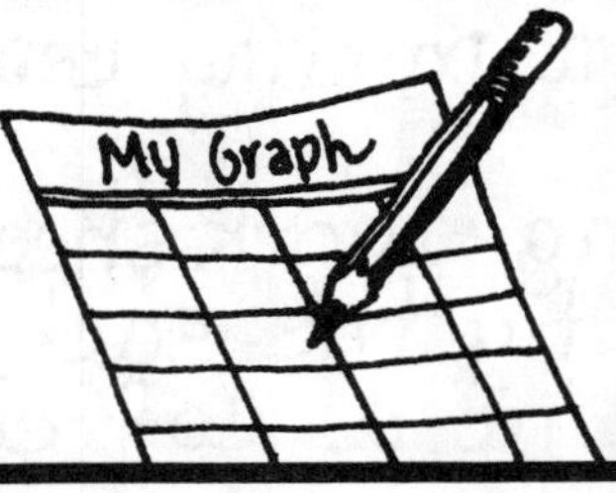


Use the dinosaur can. Sort the dinosaurs in the can by your own grouping. Make a graph to show what you discover.

Bring a shoebox from home. Make a dinosaur scene inside. Use clay to make dinosaurs. Cut trees, mountains, clouds from construction paper.

# MATERIALS FOR DINOSAUR CENTER

1. Dinosaur contract for each student.

2. Mini filmstrip-viewing center set up in the classroom. A filmstrip review worksheet for each student. Any good filmstrip on dinosaurs could be used.

3. Duplicate an adequate number of pages of the dinosaur shape for student booklets. If possible use green paper for the pages of the booklet and orange construction paper for the cover. To eliminate facial features from booklet pages, make a second stencil containing only the outline of the head.
   Provide scratch paper for story drafts. Have scissors, pencils, crayons, and a stapler available.

4. Have Danny and the Dinosaur by Sid Hoff (or a similar book of your choice) available. For non-reading students, you may tape record the story. Students may follow along as they listen. Assemble materials for art project and place in painting center.

5. Provide adequate number of graphing worksheets. Plastic dinosaurs can be purchased by the sack at most variety stores. Place them in a coffee can that has been decorated.

6. Have extra shoeboxes available. Provide clay, various colors of construction paper, scissors, paint, crayons, glue, Easter basket grass.

# Dinosaur Shape Book

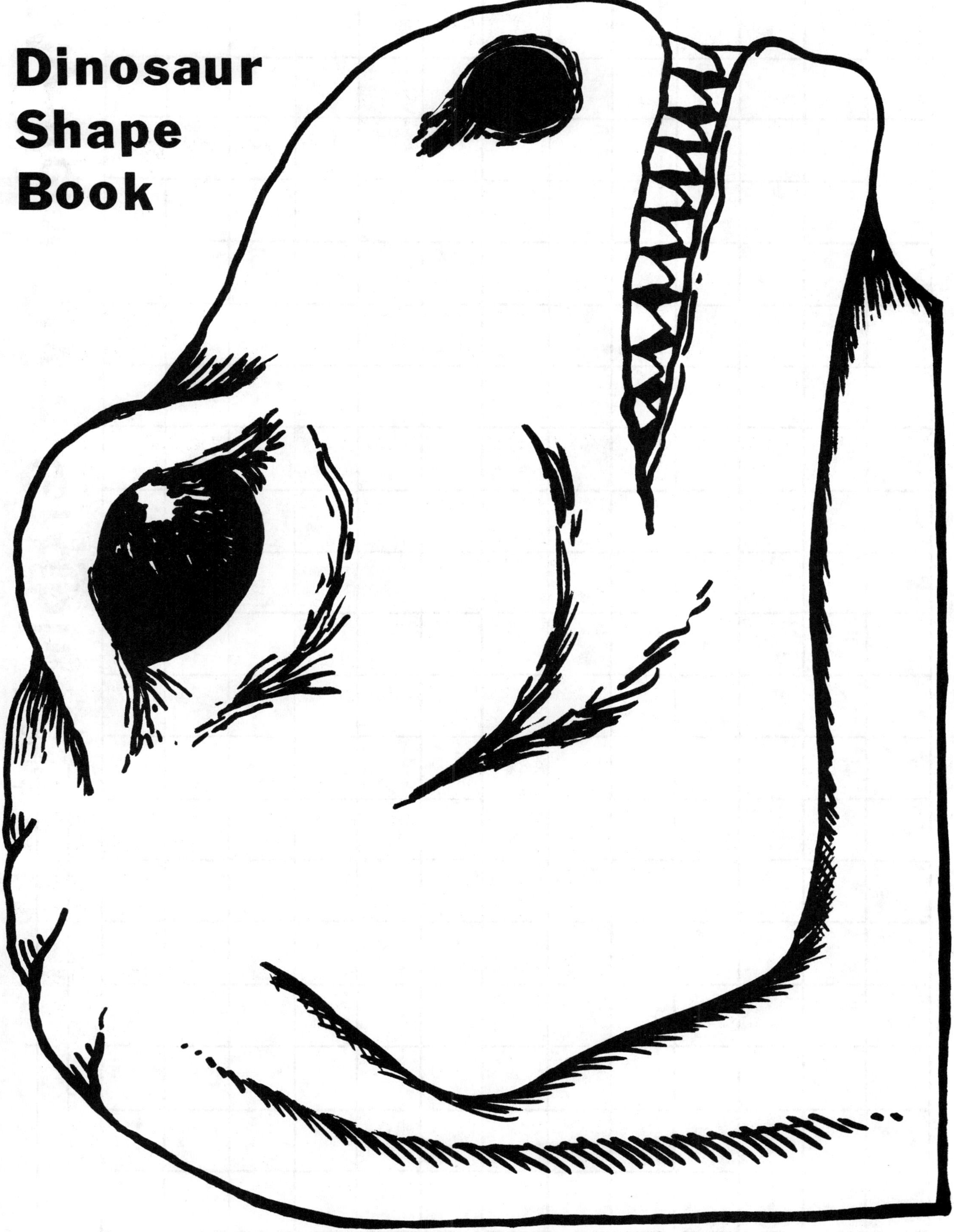

# My Very Own Graph

about ______________________

by ______________________

**SPECIAL AWARD TO**

____________________________

**for an outstanding report!**

THANK YOU

It is always nice to have awards and certificates at a center. They provide extra motivation, as well as adding a humanistic touch.

# DISPLAY ...

The center display for the unit should be visually attractive and appealing. Ideally it should be "set-up" in a corner of the classroom near a bulletin board so the students art work, contracts, and worksheets can be displayed. It should be accessible to an electric outlet for the tape recorder, filmstrip viewer, or record player.

## BULLETIN BOARD

The bulletin board should be a colorful room addition. Bright, colorful butcher paper or fabric, provides a nice background. Student art projects should become a part of the bulletin board. Add appropriate pictures and charts from magazines. Use manila folders or cereal boxes to hold student contracts and worksheets.

## SUPPLIES

All supplies needed should be located in the center area. This reduces movement in the classroom. Orange juice cans, covered with fabric or contact paper, make good pencil holders. Baby food jars are great for holding paint. Coffee cans covered with fabric or construction paper are excellent for storing small items. On the outside of any container, print the word identifying the object. You may also wish to draw a picture of the object or trace the outline.

# OTHER MATERIALS

Many centers will require the following items. Always have them handy. Store in plastic dishpans.

ART SUPPLIES - CONSTRUCTION PAPER - CRAYONS
FABRIC SCRAPS - WALLPAPER - SCRAP PAPER

Shape books can serve as a tremendous incentive for creative writing. The shape should depict a topic. The cover should be made of a durable material (tagboard, construction paper that has been laminated). Children can make covers by tracing around a cardboard pattern. Pages of writing paper for each book should be duplicated. Older students or volunteer parents can "cut-to-shape."

When listening device is in a center (tape recorder, record player, headphones, listening post) students should have previous experience using them. The use and care of any such item can be a large group lesson, but then allow each student a test run. You may wish to train two students to be "AUDIO-VISUAL EXPERTS" and allow them to instruct other students.

Visual displays on the topic of any center should be available. These can include books, filmstrips, pictures, and charts. Check your public library system to find additional audio-visual aids.

Empty ice cream cartons make excellent chart and paper holders. Cover with bright self-adhesive paper.

To make book racks, cut cardboard cartons from the grocery store, diagonally on top from back to front. Paint or cover with self-adhesive paper.

# CENTER CHECKLIST

TOPIC: ______________________

OBJECTIVES: ______________________

______________________

______________________

______________________

______________________

BULLETIN BOARDS and DISPLAYS: ______________________

______________________

______________________

VISUAL AIDS (films, charts, pictures): ______________________

______________________

______________________

______________________

______________________

| LIBRARY BOOKS: | POEMS/SONGS: |
|---|---|
| ______________________ | ______________________ |
| ______________________ | ______________________ |
| ______________________ | ______________________ |
| ______________________ | ______________________ |

| MATERIALS NEEDED: (Art Supplies) | (Worksheets and Learning Materials) |
|---|---|
| ______________________ | ______________________ |
| ______________________ | ______________________ |
| ______________________ | ______________________ |
| ______________________ | ______________________ |
| ______________________ | ______________________ |

SPECIAL EQUIPMENT: ______________________

______________________

______________________

______________________

CENTER ACTIVITIES:

MATH ______________________________

READING ______________________________

WRITING ______________________________

ART ______________________________

OTHERS ______________________________

GROUP ACTIVITIES (art, dramatics, stories, etc....)

SPECIAL ACTIVITIES (field trips, guest speakers)

SUPPLIES (needed from home) REMEMBER!!

# Parent Involvement

Inform your parents about your new centers by sending a simple note. Parents can be a tremendous resource for supplies, help and guest speakers.

Dear Parent,

We are beginning a study of dinosaurs on Monday, October 7. The children learn about these extinct animals. How large were they? Where did they live? How were they similar? What did they eat? These are just a few of the questions we will explore.

Could you please help your child prepare a brief oral report? The report should be just two or three minutes long. This report will help your child to express himself/herself more effectively. It will also be an opportunity for him/her to gain confidence in his/her ability to talk before a group.

Your child has chosen to talk about the ________ ____________________ dinosaur. Some of the things he/she might like to tell us include:

a) the size (length, height and weight).
b) What the dinosaur liked to eat.
c) Where the dinosaur lived (climate, area).
d) What happened to the dinosaur?

Any pictures, toys or books about the dinosaur could be shown during the talk.

Your child's report day is ____________________.

THANK YOU FOR YOUR COOPERATION!

____________________

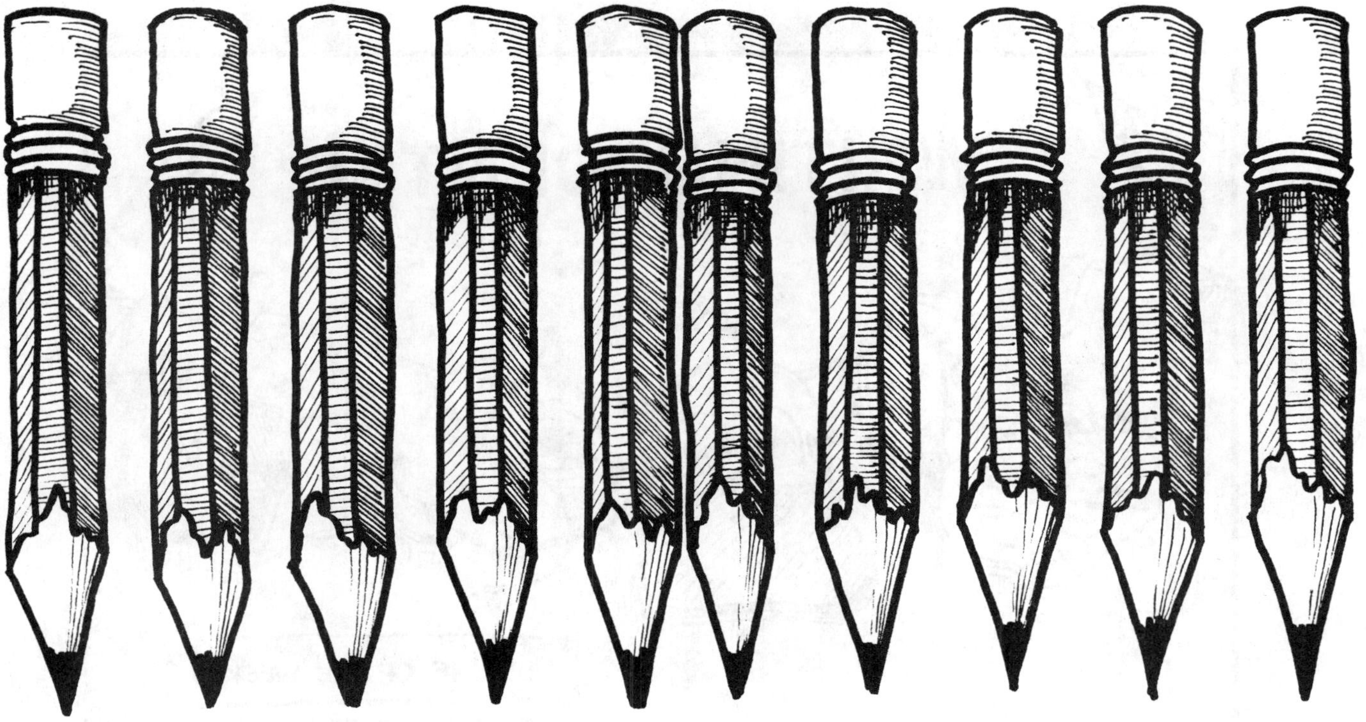

# LANGUAGE ARTS

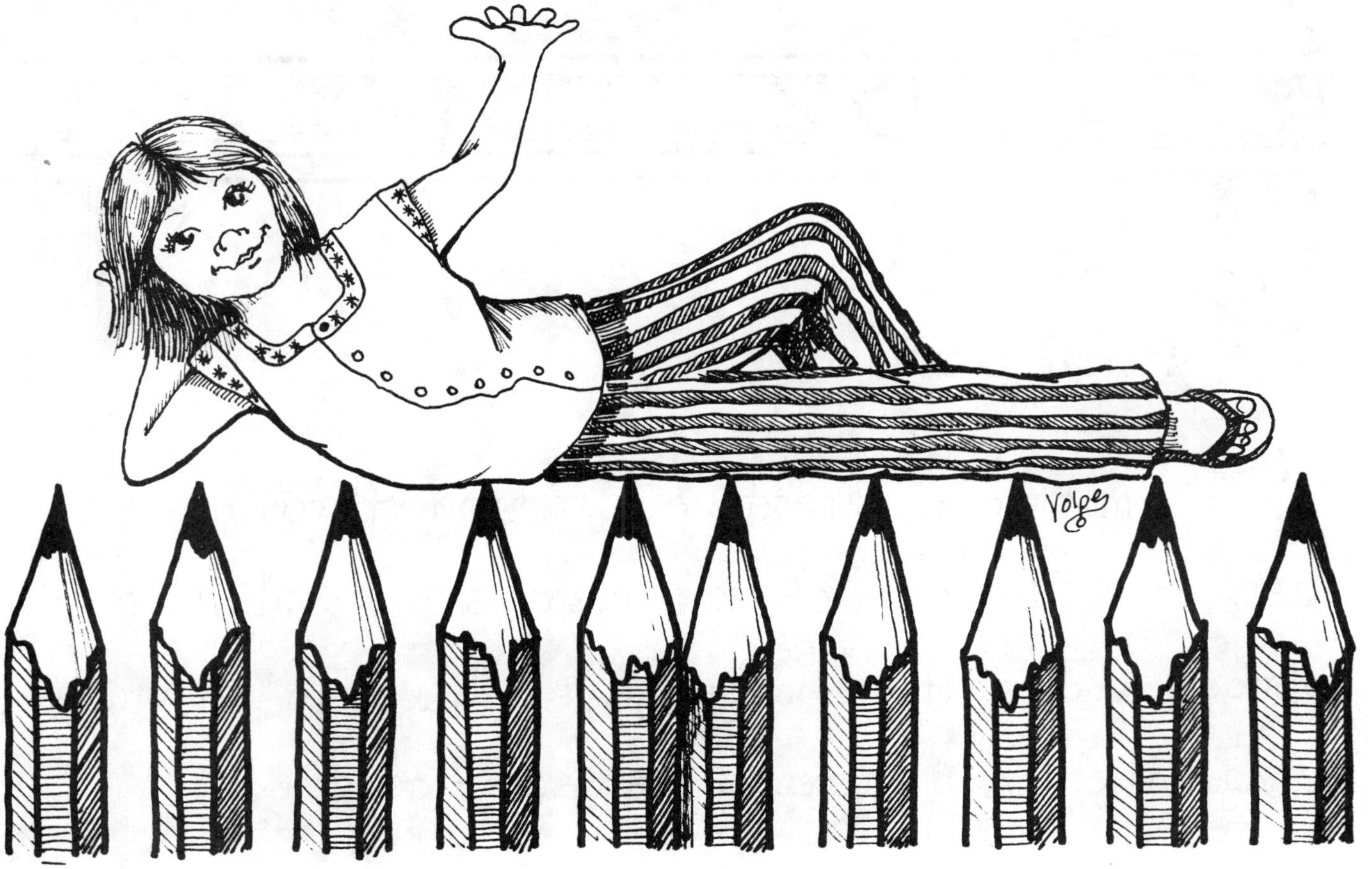

## PURPOSE

To motivate creative writing through the use of a variety of experiences. To develop verbal and written language skills. To stimulate imagination and increase self-confidence.

## PROCEDURE:

The writing center can be set up in the classroom as a temporary or permanent center. The writing center also may serve as part of the daily or weekly classroom curriculum, as well as being an enrichment area that children may use when they complete their work. As with all other centers, the writing center should be adapted to meet the teachers' and students' needs. Time schedules, and frequency of use, can vary as greatly as one hour each day to fifteen minutes each month. Once you set up your schedule, don't be afraid of rescheduling and altering the plan. Constant evaluation is part of any center.

Find a location in the room that will be convenient for use. Provide a colorful display to help motivate students about the topic. How large the space should be is determined by the number of children you plan to have use the center at the same

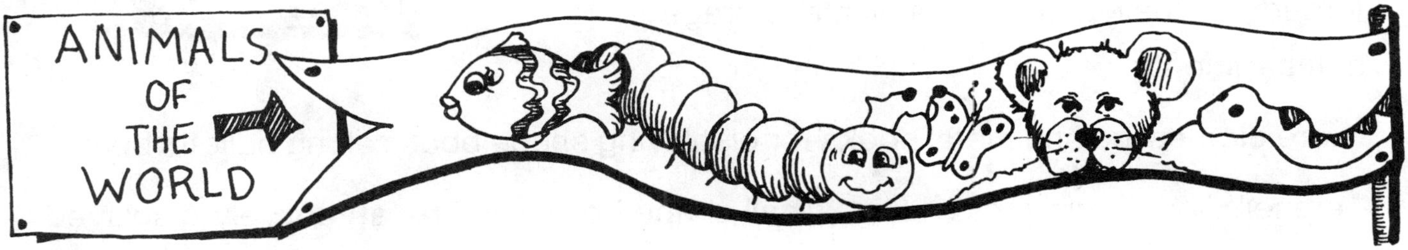


time. You may wish to make a number notation on the corner of the display, to denote to the class, the maximum number of students who can work at the center at any one time.

## MATERIALS:

The amount of material needed at the center also will be determined by how many children you plan to have use the area at one time. This number should be kept in mind as you begin to gather the supplies. Display materials so that children can put them back in an orderly fashion easily. Some materials you might need include:

* pencils (can be stored in a vegetable soup can with the top removed).
* paste (convenient for storage in baby food jars).
* scissors (can be stored in a basket or in an egg carton turned upside down).

* magazines for children to cut apart and find pictures they can write stories about (can be stored in a covered box or upright in a covered ice cream carton).

* writing paper - store in box lids and cover lids with contact paper or colorful wrapping paper. Plastic vegetable bins and tubs are also useful for storing all kinds of supplies and materials.

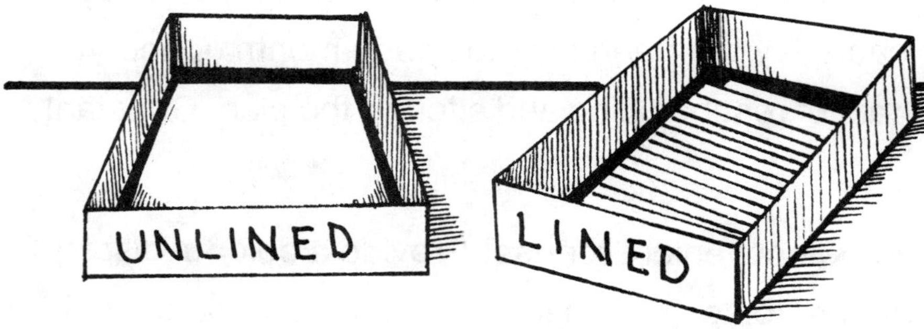


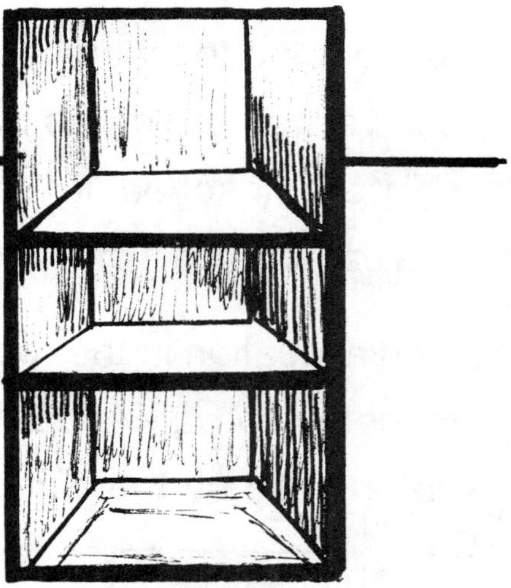

Boxes with cardboard dividers can be turned on their sides for multiple storage compartments.

* wire clothesline and metal hooks for displaying shape books along bulletin board.

* erasers, pens, crayons, rulers, small shape books can be attractively displayed in a material holder. Stitch material pockets around a heavy piece of material, such as denim, and tack up near the center.

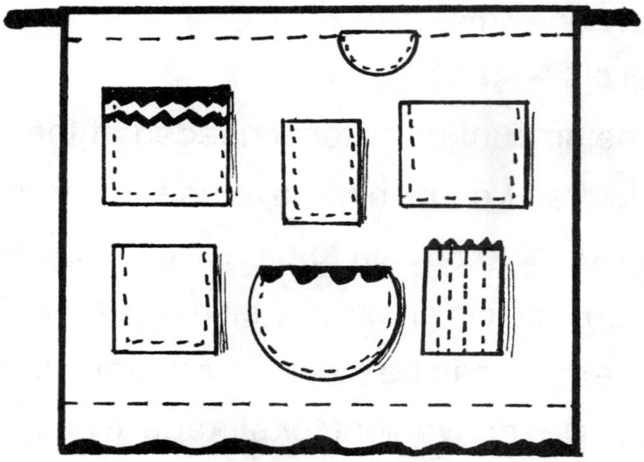

A shoe holder can also be excellent storage compartment for odds and ends.

* blank writing books

* shape books

# SHAPE BOOKS

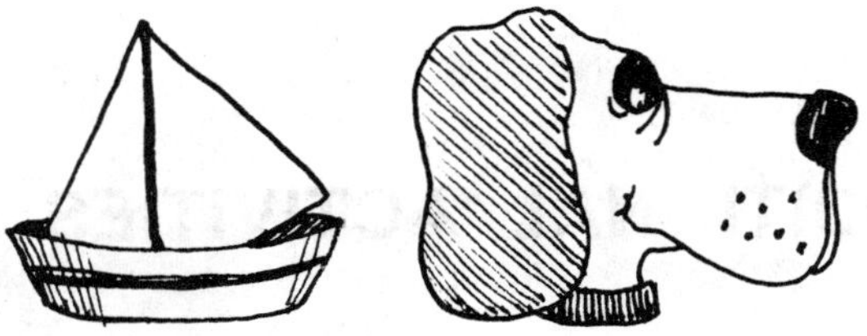

Shape books are colorful additions to the classroom and can be made easily. Coloring books, purchased at variety stores, contain many pictures that can be used for these writing shape books. Simple, large shapes, work the best. Trace around the shape onto a doubled piece of colored construction paper. Outline the shape with a felt marking pen. Cut around the shape to form the back and front cover of the writing book. Cut several pieces of writing paper from the same pattern. Staple the writing paper between the cover. Title the book if you wish, and it is ready for students to choose and use.

Display the shape book along a clothesline wire that can be hung at the back of the writing center. Children can choose which book to write in, then return the book to the wire. Several students can work to complete one book, or each student can choose his own.

To keep track of which books individual children have used, you may wish to make up a Shape Book Contract for each child. Draw a small sample of each book on the contract. As the child writes in each book, he colors that shape on his contract.

As children complete each writing book, it can be placed in the "Classroom Library" at a special table or bookcase marked "Library." Children can "check out" the cherished writing books to bring home to share and read with their families. Insert a library pocket and index card in each book. Checked out cards can be kept inside a small box. A classroom librarian may become a regular classroom monitor to supervise the class library.

## ADDITIONAL ACTIVITIES

As the teacher finds it appropriate, additional activities may be set up at the center. These changes should be explained to the children at class-meeting time. New additions to the center may be gradually introduced to the children. With each new activity, explain not only how the activity should be done, but how the activity should be stored. There will need to be discussion about record keeping.

## GRAB BAG

The Grab Bag activity may be, like all other activities, a permanent or temporary addition to the center. The Grab Bag can be made from a paper bag, or sewed from material with cording, pulled around the top to open and close. Make sure the grab bag is dark colored so the objects cannot be seen before children reach inside. Blindfolds are optional--but helpful.

Put a small object in the bag. Children come to the center and put their hands inside the bag and attempt to discover what the object is. The writing assignment is for them to write in a blank writing book or on writing paper **how the object feels.** This will be difficult for many children as you begin the assignment. Improvement will come with practice. Tell students that, by reading their description, a person should be able to guess what the object is without seeing or feeling it.

# what comes next?

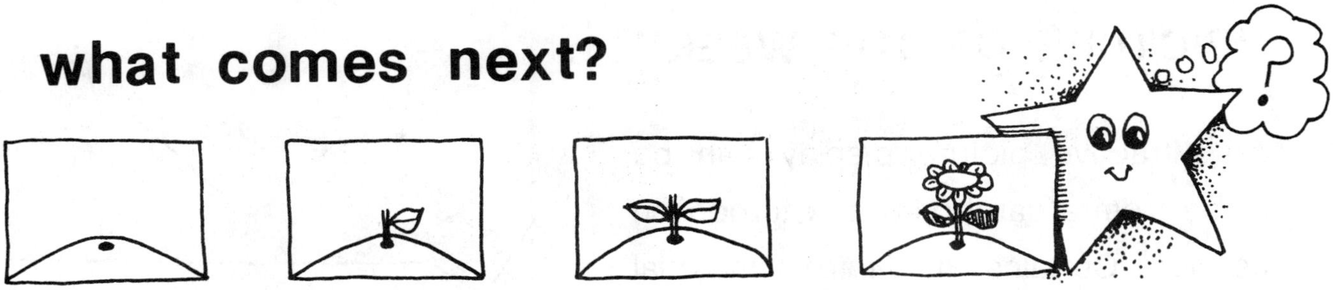

Old workbooks are a great souce of picture sequences. Cut them apart and mount them on heavy paper. Put each set in an envelope. The child chooses an envelope, and attempts to put the pictures in order, according to what happened first, second, third, and fourth. He is then to write the story on paper, providing the written narrative. As a variation to the activity, you may substitute a blank card for the fourth picture in the sequence, so the children will have to predict the ending.

## listening time

How often have we listened to a popular new song and been unable to explain what the song is about? We really didn't focus in on the words of the song. Have a child bring in a "song-of-the-week." The song should be a current popular song. Set up a phonograph and listening phones and you are ready. Children are to listen to the song and become song interpreters by writing down what the song is about.

## old shoes!

Props are fun for children to write about. You or the children can take turns bringing in an odd pair of shoes. Try to include as many different kinds as possible. Children are to write a story about who the make-believe person was that wore the shoes.

## "PICTURE OF THE WEEK"

An attractive picture display can be made from a cardboard box turned on its side. Curtains, made from material and strung across the top opening of a box on a dowel, can open and close. In the back portion of the box, choose a magazine picture to pin up for the children to write about. The picture display can be hung on the bulletin board in the writing center area. Pictures also could include selections from children's art work.

## "FRIEND OF THE WEEK"

A different friend each week can become a writing topic. A self-portrait may be drawn by the child, or real photographs of the child brought from home, may be displayed in a paper frame. Children write such things as why this person is a friend, what they have learned about him, things he likes to do, or physical descriptions of him.

## "STORY OF THE DAY"

Be sure to set aside a special place in your room for the "Story-of-the-Day." A special time each day may be set aside for authors to read their current writing creations. The class may then vote on the best "story-of-the-day" which is then hung in an honored place in the classroom.

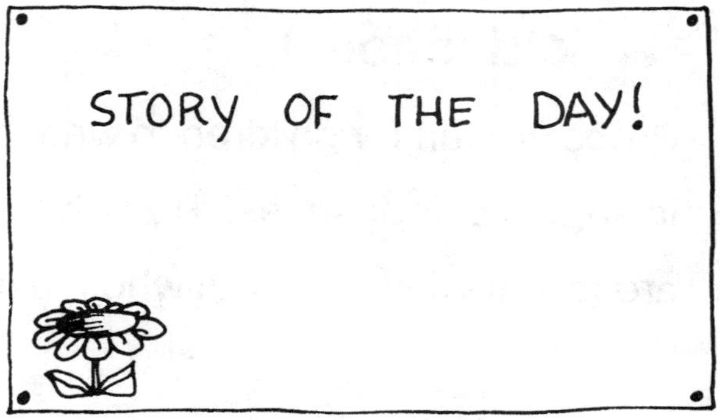

# PROPS, PROPS, PROPS.....

Other writing experiences can include props. Some things you and your students might enjoy using include:

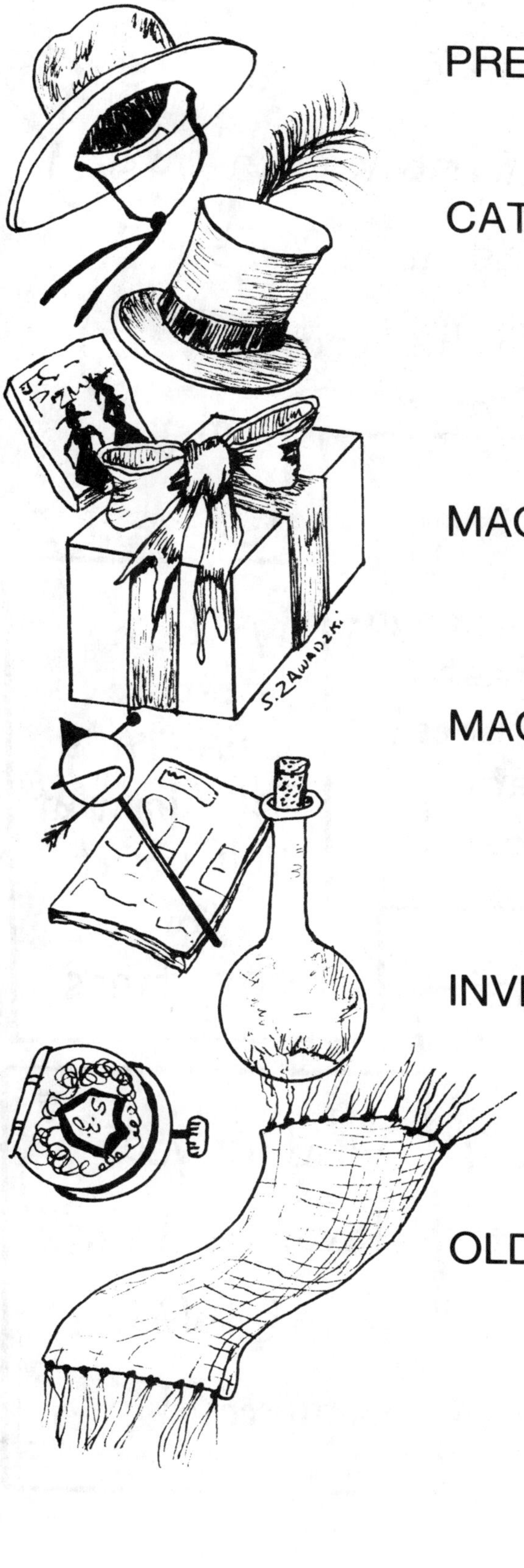


**HATS!** Children can write about the kind of person who would wear the hat.

**PRESENTS** Bring a beautifully wrapped package. Children can describe what they think (or would like to think) is in the package.

**CATALOGS** Children can leaf through and decide which thing they would like to have and why. You might set a price limit so the children will have to use adding concepts to figure out which things they can purchase.

**MAGIC WAND** Make a wand from a foil roll and attach a foil star on the end. Children may make magic wishes with it. What would they wish for?

**MAGIC CARPET** Bring in a small rug. Explain to the children that at night the carpet flies magically anywhere they want it to. Where would they like to take it?

**INVISIBLE OBJECT** Bring in a jar. Tell the children there is something inside the jar that only fairies can see. To us, it's invisible. What do they think it could be?

**OLD WATCH** Bring in an old watch that will not run. Children are to write about when they think the watch stopped. What period of time did it stop, and what was happening at the time?

# WRITING CARDS

Print each activity on a 4"x6" index card. Be sure to number each card. Keep the cards in a file box in the writing center.

**1**

Describe yourself. What do you look like? What do you do? Write it down.

**2**

Cut a picture from a magazine. Paste it on a sheet of paper. Write about it.

**3**

Write a letter to SANTA. Tell him what you want for Christmas.

**4**

What is your favorite television show? Why? Tell about it.

**5**

A magic fairy just granted you any wish. What did you wish? What happened?

**6**

Write a story about what you want to be, when you get older.

**7**

What is your favorite thing to eat? Write a commercial.

**8** A friend gives you $100. What will you do with it?

**9** Pretend that you have a robot that can do anything. What do you want him/her to do?

**10** A spaceship arrives at your doorstep. The door opens. What do you see?

**11** You wake up to find footprints on your front lawn. What made them?

**12** Write about a scary time — real or make-believe.

**13** Write a story about your best friend. What do the two of you do?

**14** A time capsule takes you back to the time of dinosaurs. What happens?

**15** If you could be any animal which animal would you choose to be? WHY?

**16** What machine are you most like? WHY?

**17** Write about a special person in your life. Why is this person special?

**18** Pretend you are the teacher. What would you teach?

**19** Write about what makes you happy.

**20** Write about a dream you nad once upon a time.

**21** What is the best book you have ever read? Why did you like it?

**22** Write about what makes you sad.

**23** A magic carpet arrives at your doorstep. Where does it take you?

# MY WRITING CONTRACT

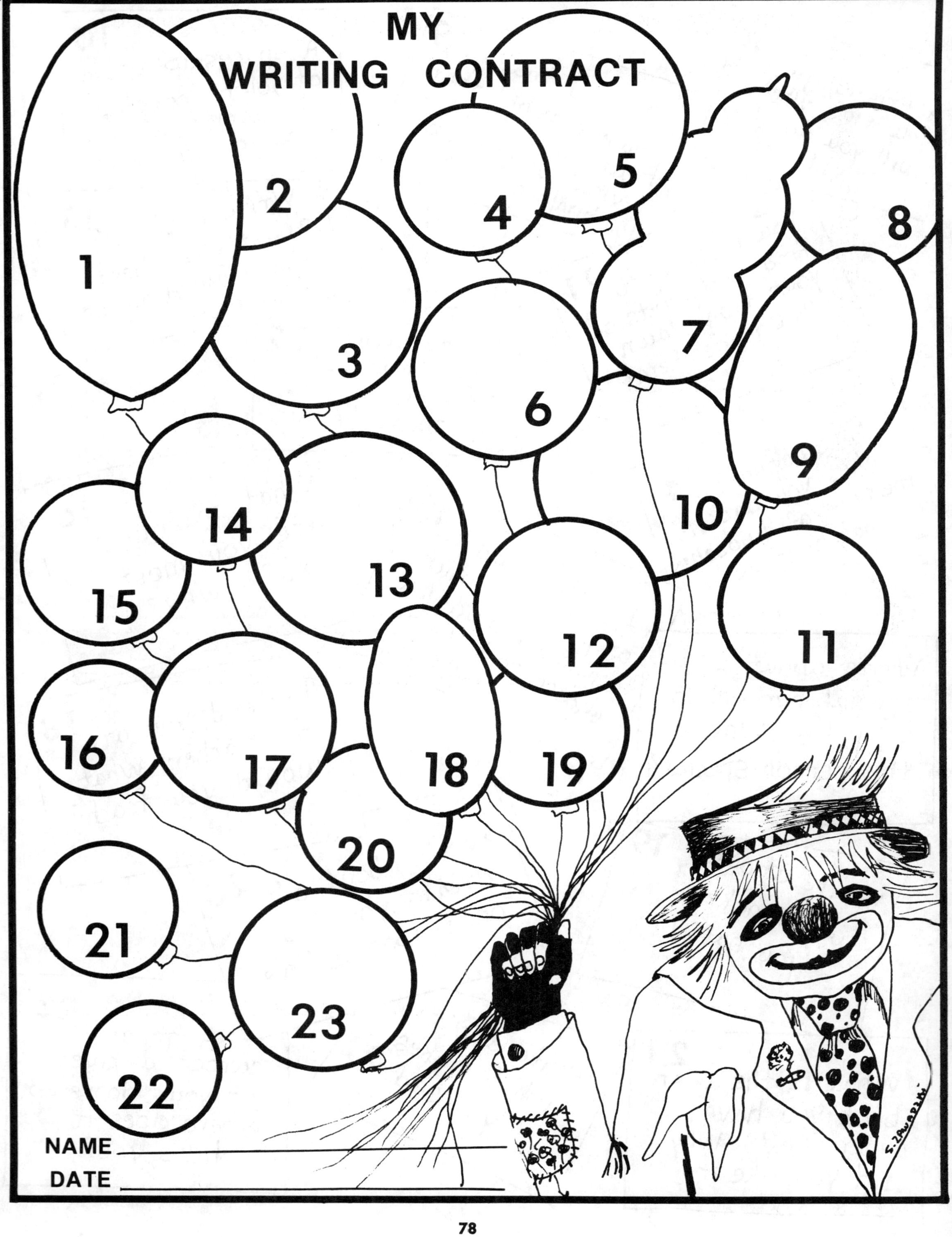


NAME ______________________________

DATE ______________________________

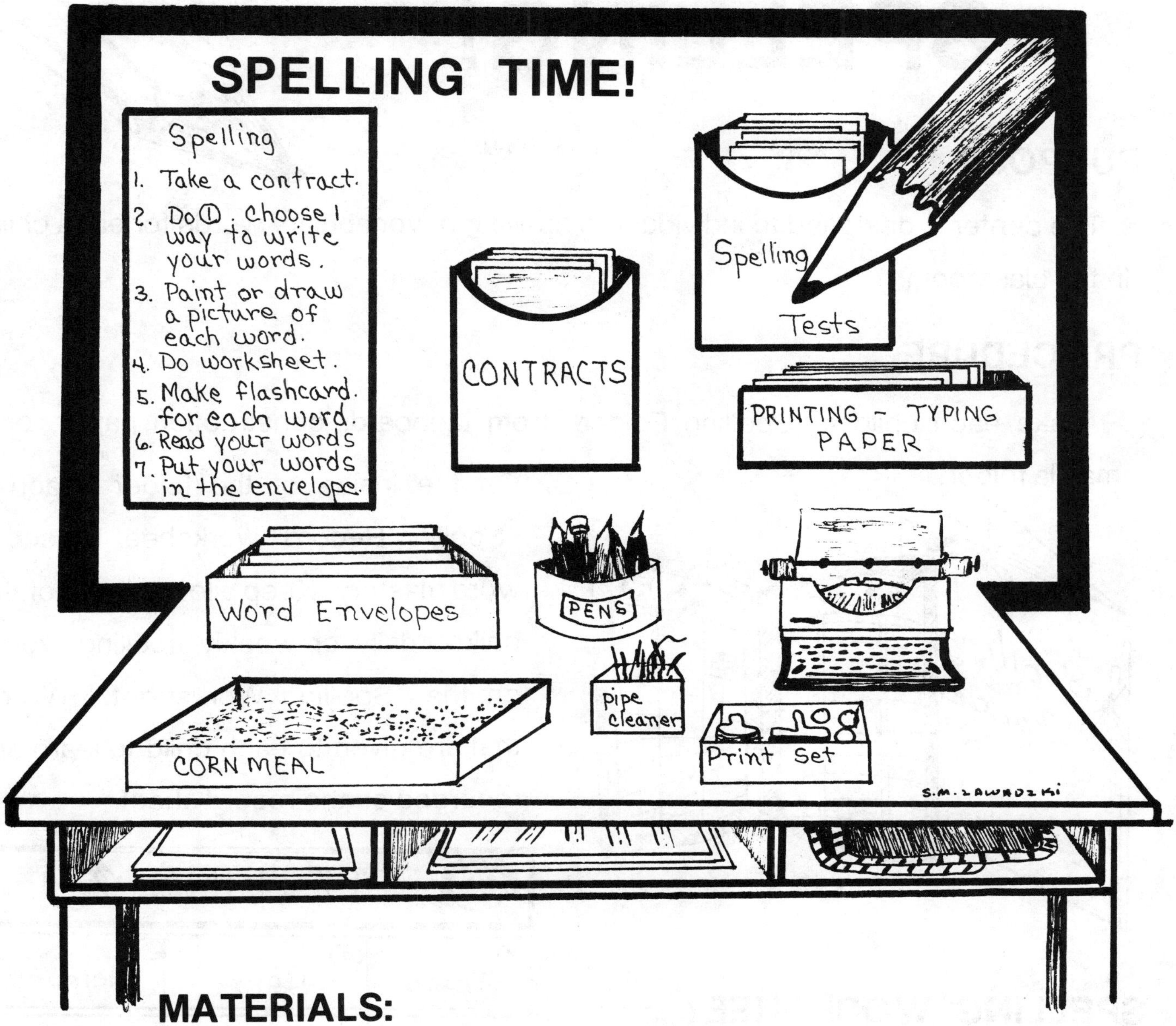


## MATERIALS:

- stamp pad and printing set of alphabet
- typewriter
- chalkboard (lap size) and chalk
- pipecleaners in a box
- cornmeal in a box lid
- 2" x 4" flashcards
- painting center or easel (paints, brushes, crayons, pencils)
- writing paper, drawing paper
- 6½" x 9" envelopes _ 1 per child
- Spelling test sheets, worksheets
- Spelling record sheet _ 1 per child
- folder _ 1 per child

# SPELLING!

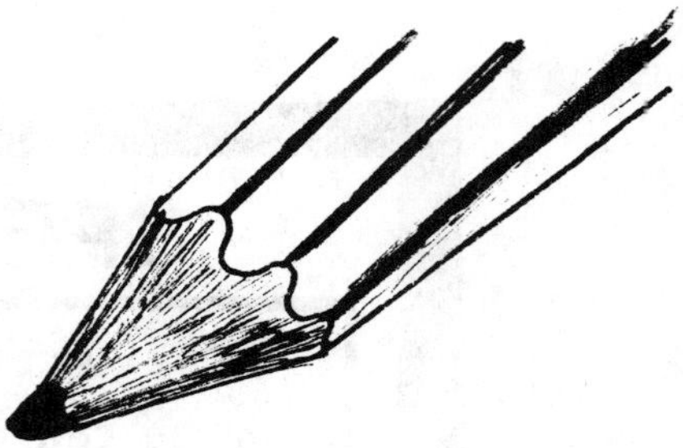

## PURPOSE

The center is designed to individualize spelling or vocabulary words for each child in the classroom.

## PROCEDURE

Make each child a "Spelling Folder" from tagboard, construction paper, or a manila folder.

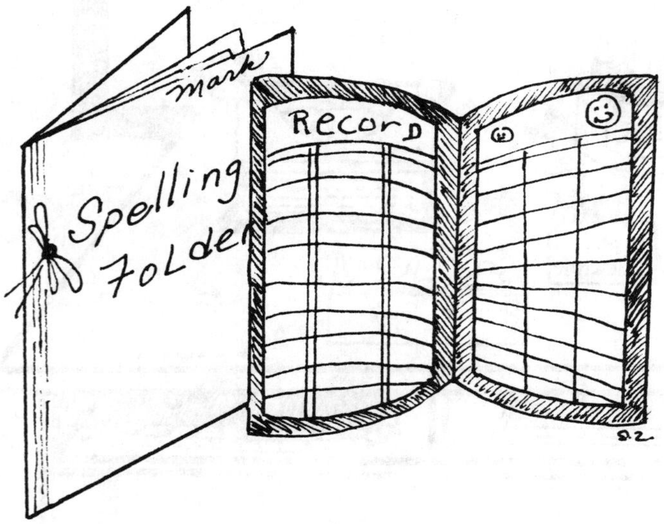


On the inside of the folder attach a "Spelling Record" worksheet to record word mastery. Keep a loose copy of the child's daily or weekly spelling words on the "Spelling Worksheet." Words that are given to each child to learn are recorded on the record sheet.

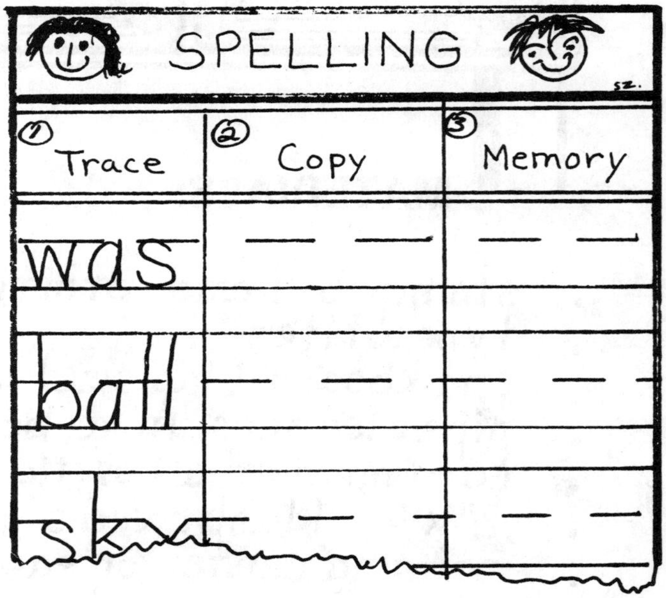


## SPELLING WORKSHEET

The Spelling Worksheet tells the child which spelling words he/she will work on for the day or week (depending on the level of your children). As progress is noted, the worksheet can be lengthened to include more words. As you observe a child having difficulty with a reading word, (during free reading, on a task card, in a story he is writing, etc.) jot it down. As you make up the spelling lists for each child, include these words in the list. Write the words under the "Trace" heading on the worksheet.

# SPELLING CENTER:

When the child is ready to work in the spelling center, he picks up his spelling folder and looks at his/her spelling words written on the "Spelling Worksheet." He/she is now ready to begin work. He/she takes a "Spelling Contract" from the center, and puts his/her name on it.

1. He/she looks at the first column on the contract and decides which fine motor task he/she will do to write the words. All the tasks are at the Spelling Center. He/she can choose to:

   print his/her words on the back of the contract.

   form the words with pipe cleaners.

   write the words on the chalkboard.

   write the words with his/her finger in the cornmeal.

   type the words on the back of the contract.

   (extra typing and printing paper is supplied at the center for free-time spelling)

   He/she indicates which task he/she chooses to do by lightly coloring the picture on his/her contract.

2. He/she then does task two on his/her contract. He/she may choose to paint a picture at the painting table, or draw a picture (paper available at the center) of all the "picture words" on his/her list. This will help him/her create his/her own image of the word. He/she should spell the words (or write a sentence using the word) by each picture. He/she then lightly colors the picture of the task he/she did on his/her contract.

3. The child is now ready for task three on his/her contract. He/she uses the worksheet already in the spelling folder that shows the spelling words. He/she proceeds in the following order:
   1. He/she carefully traces the word the teacher has written, sounding out each letter as he/she writes it.
   2. He/she copies the word under the copy column, sounding out each letter as he/she writes it.
   3. He/she folds over columns one and two on the dotted line, so they are no longer visible, and writes the word from memory. He/she unfolds the paper to see if he/she is correct.

   He/she continues the same procedure with each word. He/she colors the task number on the contract.

4. The child is now ready for task four on his/her contract. On pre-cut construction paper flash cards at the center, he/she will carefully write his/her words - one word for each card.

   He/she practices writing and reading these words throughout the day (and year).

   When the child has finished reading his/her words, he/she takes out the "Word Envelope." Inside the word envelope you may also include two smaller envelopes labeled "Words I Know" and "Words I Need to Learn." Periodically these words may be taken home to study and brought back. Parents may sign and date the front of the envelope.

   Periodically, spelling tests, (use spelling test worksheets), may be given. These may be given by a teacher, aide, cross-age tutor or peer. Words are taken from "Words I Need to Learn" packet. As mastery occurs, the teacher marks it on the record sheet and on back of flash cards. Words spelled correctly should be placed in the "Words I Know" envelope.

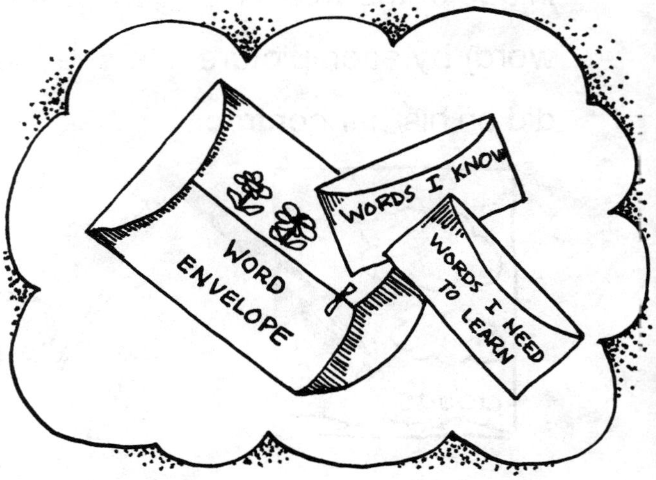

Name Date

# SPELLING CONTRACT

○ Choose 1 way to spell your words.

PRINTING 

PIPE CLEANERS 

 CHALK

CORNMEAL 

 TYPE

○ Draw or paint a picture of each word.

PAINTING 

DRAW 

○ DO WRITING PAPER

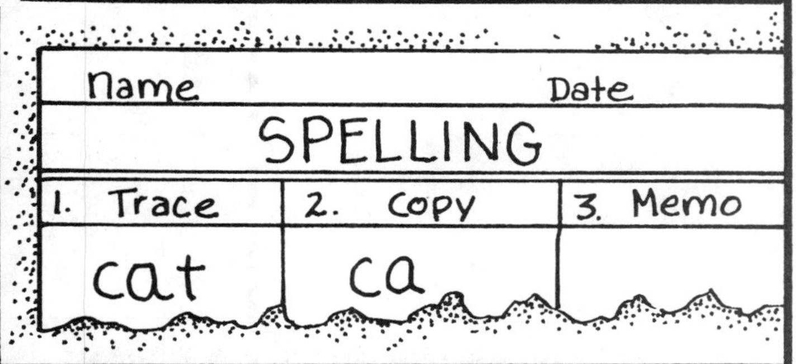


○ FLASH CARDS

a Write each word on a flashcard.

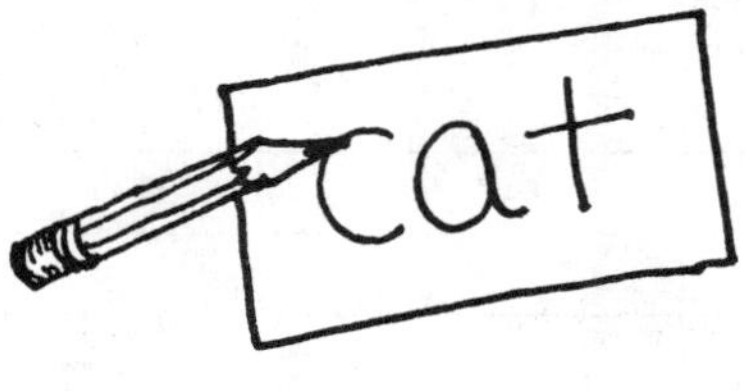


b Read your words.

c Put your words in your word envelope.

Name Date

# SPELLING

| 1 TRACE | 2 COPY | 3 MEMORY |
|---|---|---|
| | | |

NAME ______________________

# SPELLING TEST

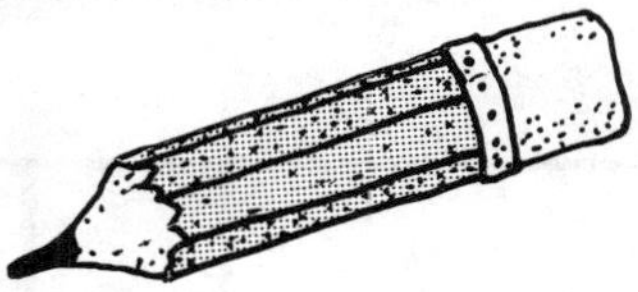

NAME ______________________

SPELLING TEST

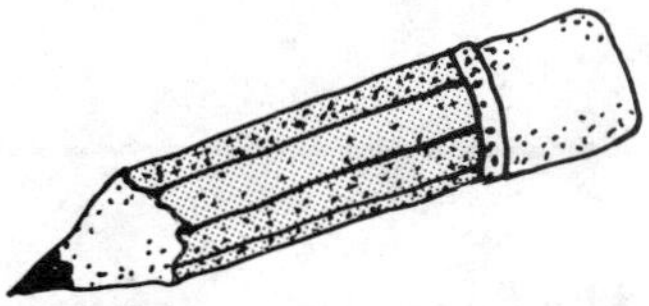

NAME ★ = mastery

# SPELLING RECORD

| | | | | |
|---|---|---|---|---|
| | | | | |
| | | | | |
| | | | | |
| | | | | |
| | | | | |
| | | | | |
| | | | | |
| | | | | |
| | | | | |
| | | | | |
| | | | | |
| | | | | |
| | | | | |
| | | | | |
| | | | | |

# INDIVIDUALIZED READING

Individualizing your reading program can prove to be a highly enjoyable, as well as a beneficial learning experience, for your children. It is also a simple process, requiring only classroom organization and time, to collect a variety of reading material.

## READING LEVELS

Begin immediately to round up reading material. Parents can be a great help and source for books. You will want a variety of material, as well as a variety of levels. As you continue your collection round-up, keep in mind the current reading levels in your room. In a first grade classroom, for instance, you will want to have picture and record books for the nonreader (Level I, one word or one sentence per page, books featuring beginning vowel sounds for the beginning reader (Level II), and books featuring more advanced vowel combinations and sight vocabulary for the advanced readers (Level III).

## CODING

For easy accessibility and convenience, books should be coded as to which level they are. Each level can be color coded in the same color and stored in a box of the same color. Grocery store boxes make attractive book displays. Cut on the diagonal from the top outside corner to six inches from the bottom of the front on both sides. Paint the box or cover it with contact paper the same color as the coding.

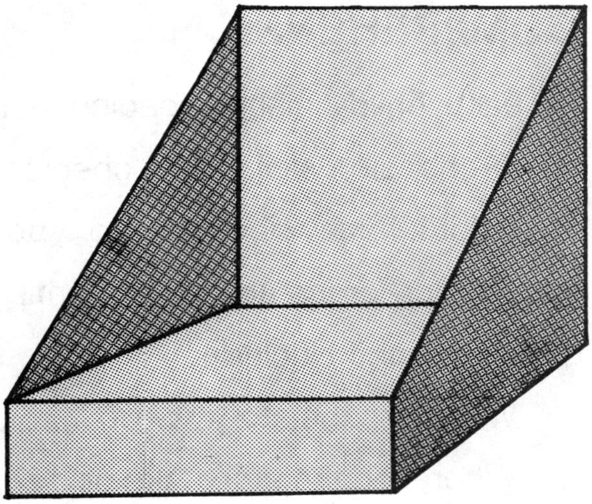

Books at each level are coded on the outside binding so that the color is visible in the display box. Colored marking pens or masking tape can be used on each book.

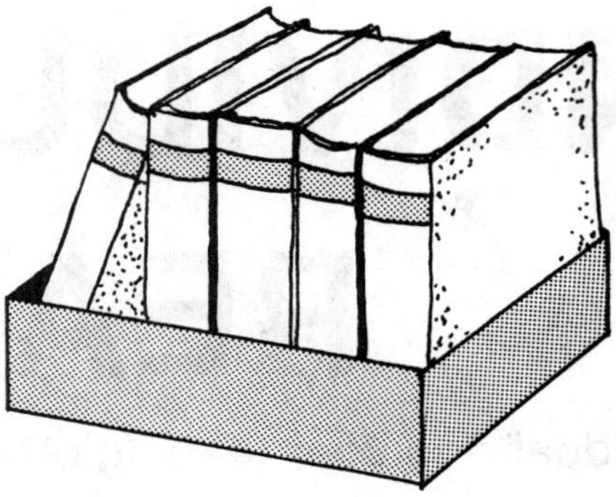

## READING FOLDER

Each child should have his/her own reading folder. These may be made from construction paper or tagboard. It may also be color coded for easy teacher reference, and also to remind the child in which box he/she is currently working. In the inside of the folder the child keeps all book reports he/she is currently writing. A reading record also is attached to one side of the folder. On this, the teacher, aide, or cross-age tutor, may note any skills the child needs to work on, or any mastery achievements. The child's current reading book also may be kept in the folder.

## COMPREHENSION

As each child finishes reading a book, he/she is checked for vocabulary and comprehension skills. This checking may be done by the teacher, aide, or cross-age tutors. It may be helpful to type a few questions on a card, that can be used by an aide or cross-age tutor, until they are confident of the procedure. Some questions might include:

What was the story about?

Where did the story take place?

Who were the main characters?

What happened in the beginning (middle, end) of the story?

Do you think the author chose a good title? Why or why not?

Can you think of another title?

Was the ending happy or sad? Why?

What did you think of the book? Why?

Would you recommend this book to a friend? Why?

The teacher may choose a few of these questions to check the child's understanding of the story. The child may then choose one favorite page to read aloud. He/she then may begin a book report. The child, at this time, can tell you which type of book report he/she has chosen to do. The book report chart may be displayed for children to choose the way he/she wishes to report. Younger children can do the first page of the written book report. As reading competency increases, the second page of the report may be included.

## VOCABULARY

The Individualized Reading Program can be the source for spelling and sight words. New words that the child encounters can be included in his/her daily (or weekly) spelling sheet. It is important to include words, that the child is learning, in his/her reading book on the "Reading Record" sheet. The teacher can easily transfer these words to his/her spelling worksheet. It is very helpful to list new vocabulary words on the inside cover of the books in which they appear. Children can then practice these words by themselves, or with teacher help, before attempting the reading. A complete list of vocabulary words, the child has mastered, will appear on the "Spelling Record" worksheet inside his/her Spelling Folder.

## PHONICS

A record of each child's phonic skills can be found on the Phonics Record. This also can be kept inside the "Reading Folder." As a new phonics skill is introduced, a notation should be made on the profile. A separate notation should be made when the skill has been mastered.

## COMPLETION

As each child finishes his/her book and report, the report should be placed inside a specially designated "Reading Box." The teacher then makes a notation on the child's Reading Record in his/her Reading Folder and on his/her weekly prescription sheet (or contract). The teacher (or the child) then chooses new reading material. A special reading award may go home to the child's parents for special recognition. These may be made in plentiful supply on a stencil and run off on construction paper. Each child may keep his/her own reading progress noted on his/her "Bookworm Chart." A part of the worm may be colored for each book read.

READING AWARD

*NOTE TO TEACHER A reward similar to the one illustrated above can be drawn and duplicated as needed.

# PHONETIC PROGRESS PROFILE

NAME ______________________

— underline = introduction O= mastery

| | | | | | | | | | | | | | |
|---|---|---|---|---|---|---|---|---|---|---|---|---|---|
| Consonants | ball b | cat c | duck d | fish f | garden g | house h | jam j | kite k | lamp l | mittens m | nest n | pig p | queen qu |
| Consonants | rug r | sun s | turtle t | vase v | wagon w | box x | yarn y | zebra z | Jack ck | phone ph | ghost gh | kw | judge dge |
| Vowel Sounds | apple ă | elephant ĕ | Indian ĭ | octopus ŏ | umbrella ŭ | apron ā | equal ē | ice ī | open ō | uniform ū | my y(i) | penny y | |
| Vowel Comb. | tree ee | eat ea | head ea | boat oa | play ay | Europe eu | vein ei | ceiling ei | rescue ue | true ue | few ew | great ea | toe oe |
| Vowel Comb. | car ar | are | her er | bird ir | corn or | ore | burn ur | light igh | cow ow | snow ow | ouch ou | soup ou | ball a |
| Vowel Comb. | raw aw | August au | oil oi | boy oy | eight eigh | chief ie | good oo | zoo oo | suit ui | mail ai | ear | | |
| Consonant Cluster | spin sp | scale sc | skate sk | small sm | swarm sw | flame fl | blame bl | claw cl | glass gl | slip sl | train tr | crash cr | dress dr |
| Consonant Cluster | fry fr | pry pr | bright br | write wr | spray spr | throw thr | scream scr | shreak shr | splash spl | squash squ | | | |
| Special Sounds Vowel-Consonant-e | shell sh | whale wh | that th | chair ch | match tch | tank nk | think th | cake a_e | athlete e_e | five i_e | rope o_e | cube u_e | type y_e |
| Special Sounds | machine ch | is s | cinch ci | cents ce | ginger gi | cage ge | know kn | sang ng | they ey | monkey ey | solve ve | school ch | |
| Suffixes | (t) ed | (d) ed | s | ing | es | er | ly | ness | less | est | ful | en | ish |
| Suffixes | n | ies | ward | ment | ous | sion | tion | self | y | ern | teen | ship | |
| Prefixes | a | im | in | re | dis | de | un | mis | pre | con | pro | en | ex |

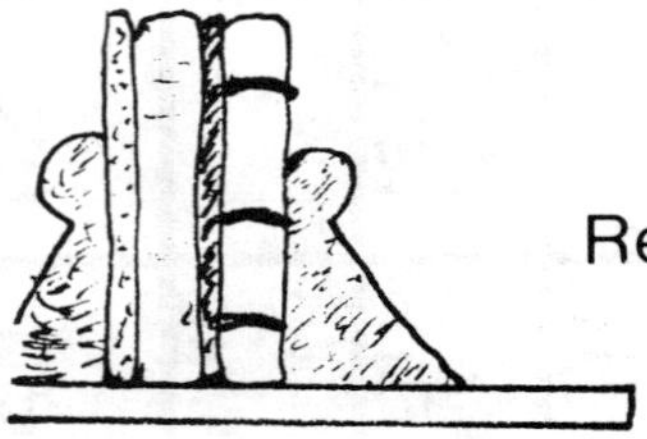

# READING RECORD

Reader ______________________________

| TITLE | AUTHOR | OBSERVATION CONCERNS | DATE START. | DATE COMPL. |
|---|---|---|---|---|
| | | | | |

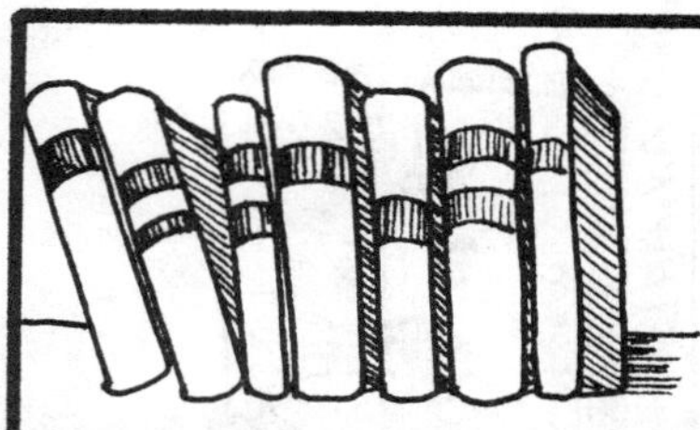

# BOOK REPORTS

Which will you choose?

# BOOK REPORT

TITLE ______________________________

AUTHOR ______________________________

REVIEWER ______________________________

**This is a picture of my favorite part:**

## Words I learned or liked are:

## This book was about:

## My rating of this book is:

# MY BOOKWORM RECORD

Bookworm______________________________

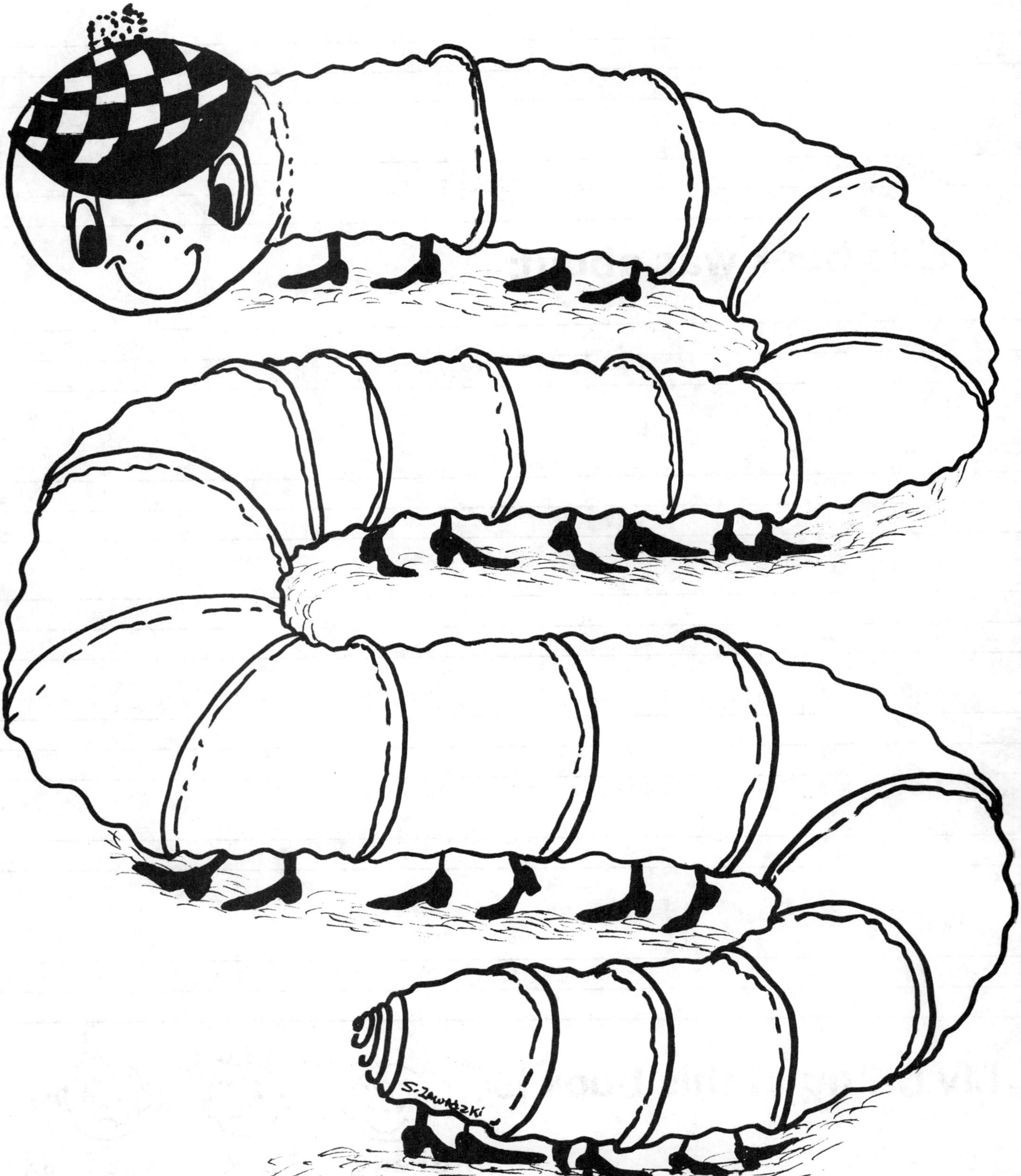

# WORD FAMILIES

## PURPOSE:

To sound out words on the basis of word families and to increase sight vocabulary.

## MATERIALS:

...... Word family contract for each child.

...... "New Reading Words" worksheets.

...... Shoe box to hold word family cards.

..... 16 sets of word family flash cards.

## PROCEDURE:

1. Child takes a word family set that he/she has not previously read.
2. He/she sounds out each new word in the set.
3. He/she chooses six "picture" words to write on his/her "New Reading Words" worksheet.
4. He/she writes the word on the left-hand column and he/she draws a picture of the word on the right-hand column. He/she continues until he/she has completed the worksheet.
5. He/she reads his/her words in the set to a teacher or aide.
6. He/she marks himself/herself off in the correct square on his/her contract.

## WORD FAMILY CARDS:

Old flash cards are ideal to use. On the back of the card, write the word family name. New initial consonants, which will form the new words, are written on flash cards, cut in half. Punch a hole in the top left-hand corner of each card and fasten the cards together with a plastic ring, yarn or pipe cleaner. The child can then leaf through the cards easily.

| | | | |
|---|---|---|---|
| 1. at<br>rat pat<br>sat that<br>flat chat<br>fat brat<br>bat scat<br>hat mat | 2. an<br>man Nan<br>fan van<br>can tan<br>ban ran<br>pan clan<br>Stan than | 3. am<br>dam slam<br>jam ham<br>cram Pam<br>clam<br>Sam<br>ram | 4. ip<br>sip ship<br>zip dip<br>rip drip<br>nip chip<br>lip whip<br>hip tip |
| 5. im<br>dim Tim<br>him skim<br>Jim grim<br>Kim brim<br>rim | 6. in<br>bin grin<br>fin skin<br>pin chin<br>tin shin<br>win thin | 7. ig<br>wig big<br>rig<br>pig<br>fig<br>dig | 8. it<br>fit pit<br>hit sit<br>kit skit<br>lit<br>bit |
| 9. ug<br>jug bug<br>rug shrug<br>mug chug<br>hug tug<br>dug | 10. ut<br>cut<br>hut<br>nut<br>rut | 11. op<br>pop shop<br>mop chop<br>cop flop<br>hop top<br>crop stop | 12. ot<br>cot not<br>dot tot<br>hot shot<br>lot got<br>pot |
| 13. en<br>ten men<br>Ken Glen<br>Ben then<br>den<br>hen | 14. ed<br>fed Fred<br>bed shed<br>Ted led<br>red fled<br>Ned | 15. et<br>wet vet<br>get pet<br>met net<br>let<br>jet | 16. ap<br>lap map<br>cap trap<br>tap clap<br>sap flap<br>rap |

# NEW READING WORDS

NAME ______________________

| WRITE THE WORD | PICTURE OF THE WORD |
|---|---|
| | |
| | |
| | |
| | |
| | |

# MY READING CONTRACT OF WORD FAMILIES

NAME ______________________ DATE ______________

| | | | |
|---|---|---|---|
| 1. at | 2. an | 3. am | 4. ip |
| 5. im | 6. in | 7. ig | 8. it |
| 9. ug | 10. ut | 11. op | 12. ot |
| 13. en | 14. ed | 15. et | 16. ap |

# WORD BLENDING CONTRACT

| | | | |
|---|---|---|---|
| ① ad<br>glad mad<br>sad lad<br>bad<br>had | ② ell<br>spell jell<br>shell fell<br>swell<br>bell | ③ ill<br>spill hill<br>mill fill<br>pill will<br>dill till | ④ ack<br>stack pack<br>track sack<br>quack back<br>black rack |
| ⑤ y<br>by cry<br>my sty<br>fly shy<br>fry dry | ⑥ ee<br>three see<br>agree bee<br>flee fee<br>tree | ⑦ ick<br>thick pick<br>wick click<br>sick trick<br>quick | ⑧ ish<br>wish<br>dish<br>fish<br>swish |
| ⑨ uff<br>stuff puff<br>bluff muff<br>cuff<br>gruff | ⑩ uck<br>struck<br>truck<br>duck<br>luck | ⑪ ank<br>tank rank<br>spank drank<br>thank<br>sank | ⑫ ink<br>blink pink<br>link wink<br>sink stink<br>think |
| ⑬ ing<br>swing ding<br>sting king<br>string ring<br>sing wing | ⑭ ang<br>clang sang<br>sprang rang<br>bang<br>hang | ⑮ atch<br>batch catch<br>patch latch<br>hatch<br>match | ⑯ unch<br>punch<br>munch<br>lunch<br>bunch |

# TYPING LAND

## PURPOSE:

To help develop sequencing skills, alphabetizing, and spelling skills. To foster fine motor development.

## MATERIALS:

Typewriter

Task cards: type each of the activities onto 4" × 6" cards. The cards should be laminated for durability. Number each card on the top right-hand corner. The cards may be kept in order by punching each card in the top left-hand corner and attaching a metal ring.

Extra typing paper

Typing contract for each child with the same number of boxes to color as task cards.

Alphabet chart for reference.

## SUGGESTED ACTIVITIES:

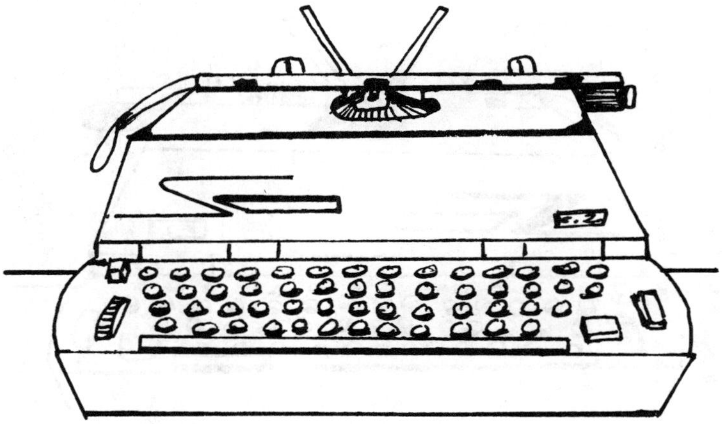

1. Type your name.
2. Type the name of your school.
3. Type the girls' names in your room.
4. Type the boys' names in your room.
5. Type the capital letters of the alphabet. (May be listed).
6. Type the lower case letters of the alphabet. (List).
7. Type the numbers as far as you can count!
8. PATTERNS
   What comes next? Type the pattern.
   abababababab__ __ __ __ __
   clclclclclcl__ __ __ __ __
   jejejejejeje__ __ __ __ __
9. PATTERNS
   Type the pattern.
   efg efg efg ef __ __ __ __ __ __ __ __
   ijk ijk ijk ij__ __ __ __ __ __ __ __
10. TYPE THE PATTERN.
    What comes next?
    ABC__
    DEF__
    HIJ__
11. TYPE THE PATTERN.
    What comes next?
    123__
    567__
    789__

12. TYPE THESE COLOR WORDS:
    red yellow
    blue green
13. SHORT A WORDS
    at Sam jam ram bat cat rat sat

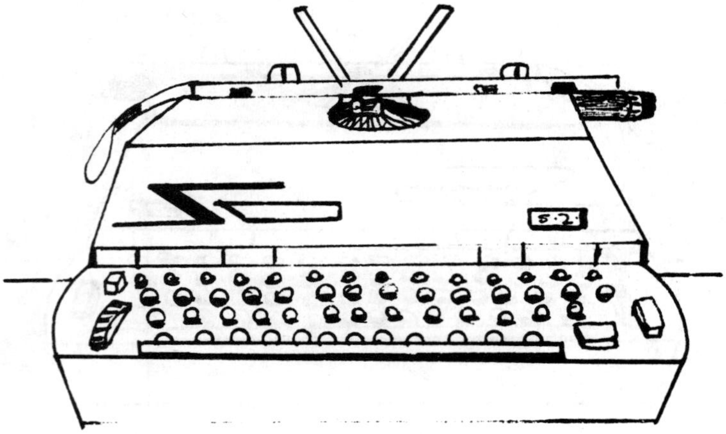

14. TYPE THIS PATTERN:
efghefghefg__ __ __ __ __
jklmjklmjkl__ __ __ __ __
qrstqrstqr__ __ __ __ __

15. WHAT IS MISSING?
a__cd__fgh__j __ __ mn
o__ __ rs__ __vwxy__

16. TYPE THE TALL LETTERS OF THE ALPHABET.
bdf__ __ __ __

17. TYPE THE SHORT LETTERS OF THE ALPHABET.
ace__ __ __ __ __ __ __ __ __
__ __ __

18. TYPE 5 WORDS FROM YOUR READING BOOK.

19. TYPE YOUR SPELLING WORDS.

20. HOW MANY?

..__ __ ..... __ __ __
. __ __ __ ... __ __ __ __
....__ __ __ __ __ __

21. WHAT COMES NEXT?
A__CDE__ __H__JKL__ __O__
QRS__ __ __WXY__.

22. NUMBERS.
1, 2, __, 4, 5, __, __, 8, __, 10

23. TYPE THE TITLE OF YOUR READING BOOK.

24. TYPE THE VOWELS.

25. TYPE THE CONSONANTS.

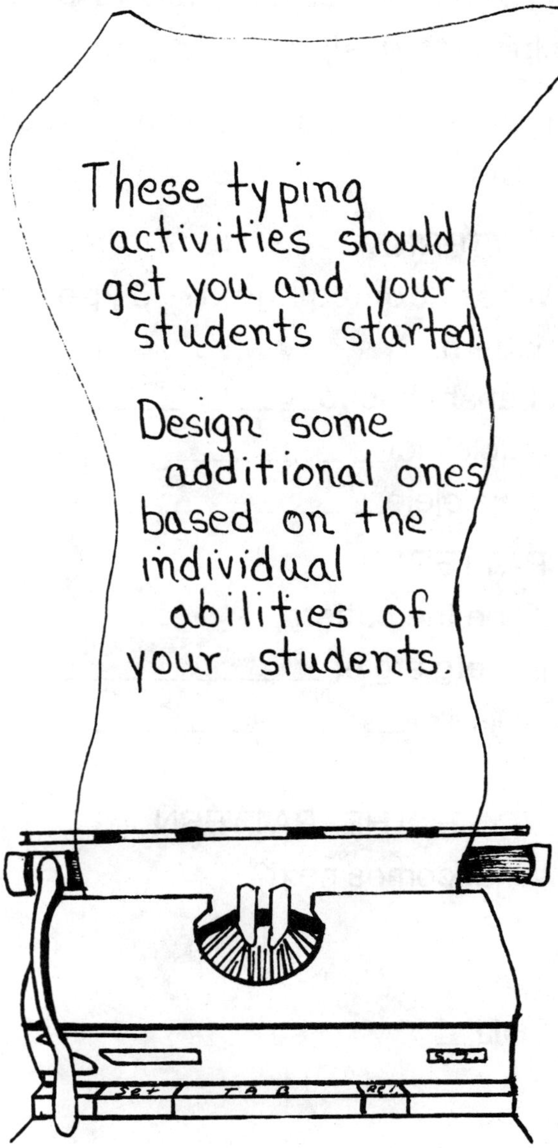

## PURPOSE:

To identify color words.

To experiment with primary and secondary color relationships.

## MATERIALS:

Large box, decorated with balloons, to be used for portable color center.

Display bulletin board (as above) with the color words written on a colored construction paper balloon depicting the color word.

Watercolor pens and sponge.

Color contract for each child.

Manila stationery envelopes.

Contact paper.

# PROCEDURE:

Make each activity as described below. Activity cards can be made on tagboard and laminated so that children may write directly on them with a watercolor pen and "erase" with a damp sponge. Place the activity cards, and any materials needed for the task, in manila envelopes. Number the envelopes on the upper right-hand corner. Some tasks may not need to be put in an envelope.

# TASKS FOR COLOR CENTER:

## 1 Color Blob Animal

You need:

paint (yellow, red, blue)

brush

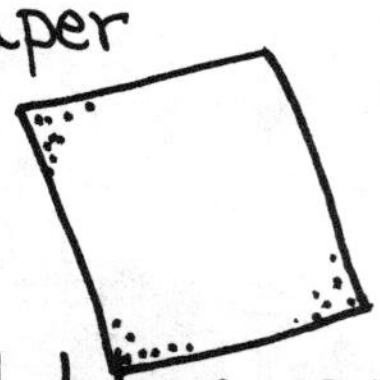
paper

crayon

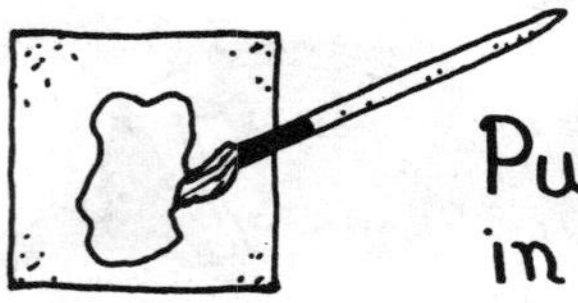

Put a blob of red, yellow and blue paint in the middle of the paper.

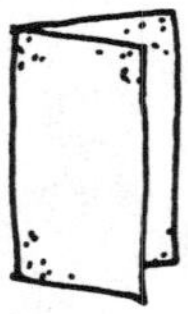

Fold the paper in half. Press together.

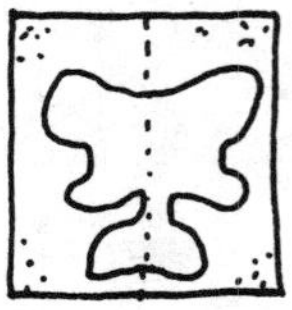

Open up and look. Can you find any <u>new</u> colors that you made?

Take a black crayon. Can you make a funny animal?

---

## 2 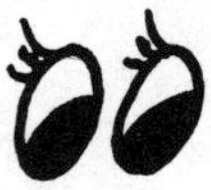 Keep Your Eyes Open!

Look carefully around the room. Find these things:

1 blue thing — 2 red things
1 yellow thing — 2 green things

## 3 Color Discovery Center

*NOTE TO TEACHER At the center you will need a medicine dropper, 3 small jars, red, yellow and blue food coloring, and a small pail of water. Be sure to color code the dots drawn on the task cards with appropriately colored pens.

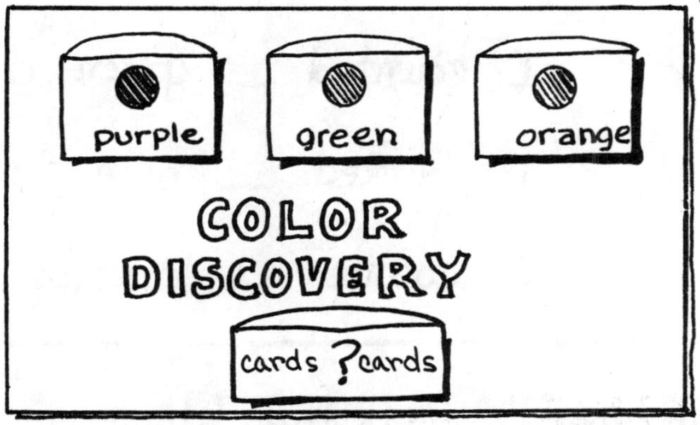


Look closely at each question card. Take one drop of each of the two colors. Drop them into the jar. What new color did you make? Put the question card in the correct envelope

question cards

## 4 EYE COLORS

| colors | 1 | 2 | 3 | 4 | 5 | 6 | 7 | 8 | 9 | 10 | 11 | 12 | 13 | 14 |
|---|---|---|---|---|---|---|---|---|---|---|---|---|---|---|
| brown eyes | | | | | | | | | | | | | | |
| blue eyes | | | | | | | | | | | | | | |
| green eyes | | | | | | | | | | | | | | |

Look carefully at the color of each of your classmate's eyes. What color are they? Show what you find on the chart.

Which color is the most?

## 5 COLOR PUZZLES

On 8" x 12" cardboard strips print a color word on the left side. On the right side make a colored circle representing the color word. Cut a jagged line in the middle. Place in activity envelope for students to match.

## 6 DINOSAURS

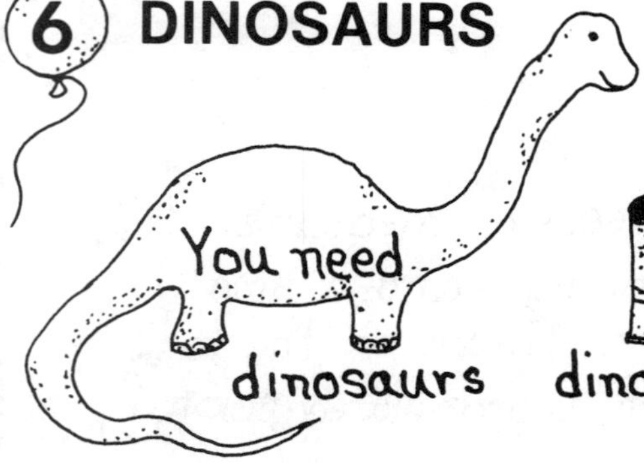

You need

dinosaurs  dinosaur can

Sort and Count

I counted __ red dinosaurs

I counted __ yellow dinosaurs

I counted __ green dinosaurs

I counted __ blue dinosaurs

I counted __ orange dinosaurs

## 7 COLOR PATTERNS

You need: Colored block cubes.

Make these patterns:

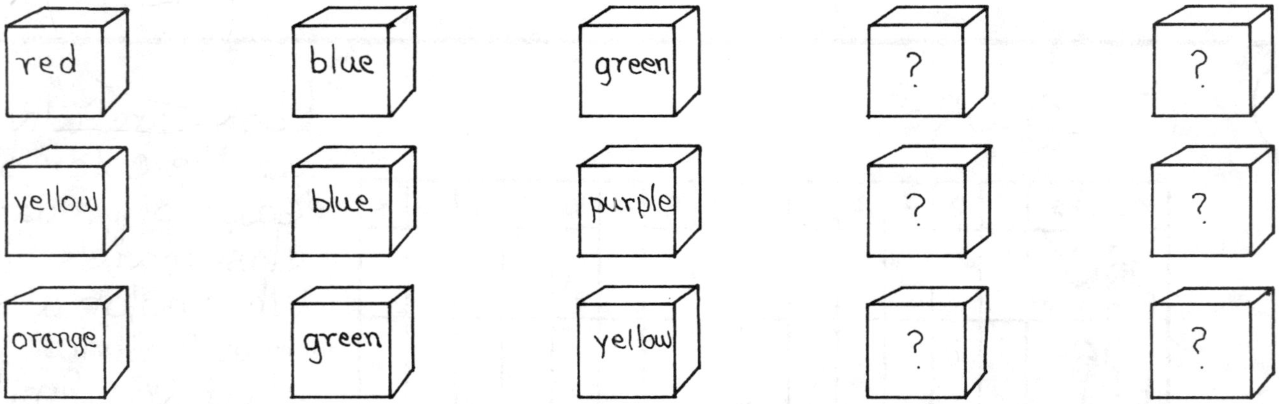


## 8 WHAT COLORS ARE YOU WEARING?

Circle the names of the colors you are wearing.

black  blue  yellow  green

brown  orange  white  red

# MATH CENTERS

# SORTING

## PURPOSE:

Sorting experiences are extremely important in forming a basis for the development of both logical thinking and mathematical concepts. It will later help children to think of all possible relationships. This center will help the child develop this foundation.

## MATERIALS:

Provide a great variety of objects to sort. Each of the objects can be placed in a coffee can which has been covered with contact paper. On the outside, list the cans contents. These cans will prove to be of tremendous value in other math tasks. Items in these cans might include different kinds of macaroni, seeds, beans, balloons, rubber bands, buttons, nuts and bolts, cards, toy cars, dinosaurs, boats, airplanes, bottle caps, pencils, lids, animals, beads, coins, trucks, tangrams. The list is endless! Cans should be accessible for frequent use.

A contract similar to the one on the next page should be provided for each child. Children sort the objects in each picture. They are to classify the objects in accordance with some property. The usual solution is to classify on the basis of shape, color or size. As children sort the objects in a can, they are to put together all the objects that are alike in some way. Large lengths of yarn knotted together form excellent loop groupings. These can be stored easily. A child must tell you his "rule" of sorting before he can receive a check mark, i.e., if he was sorting the dinosaur can by color, he can verbalize, "these are alike because they are green, these are the red dinosaurs... these are yellow, etc."

# SORTING CONTRACT

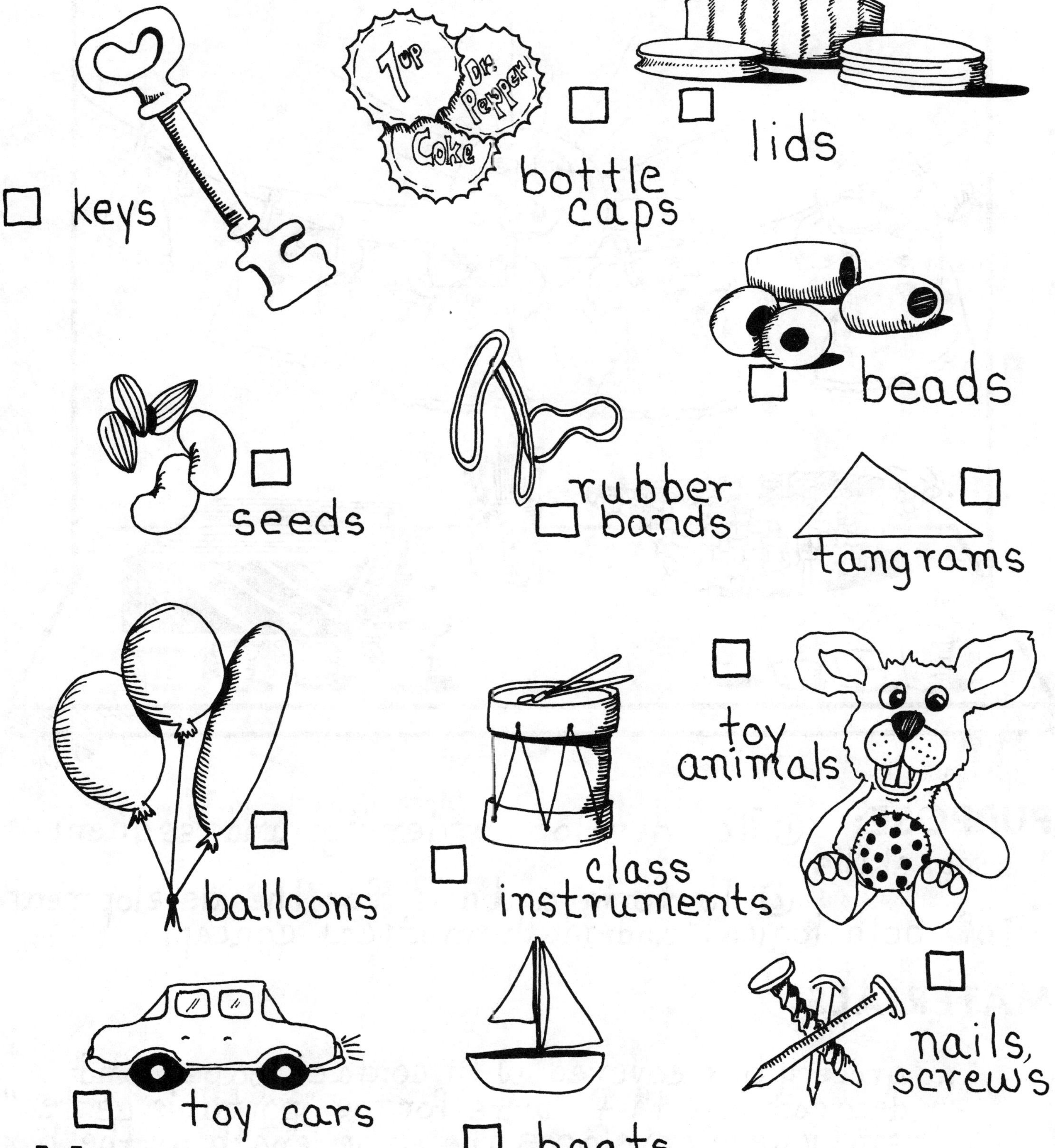


**Name** ______________________________

# ORDERING

**PURPOSE:** ① To develop ordering and sequencing skills.

② To form a basis for the development of both logical and mathematical concepts.

**MATERIALS:**

...... grocery box covered with contact paper and decorated with flowers for the "portable center."
...... stationery envelopes the same length as the box to hold materials and activity cards.
...... copy of ordering contract for each child.

**ORDERING LENGTH**

Place 8 pieces of rug yarn of varying lengths in the activity envelope. Children are to order their lengths from shortest to longest.

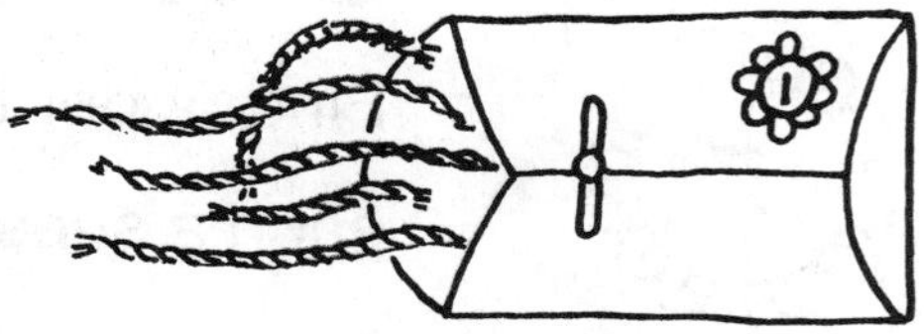


**ORDERING HEIGHT**

Find 5 friends in the room. Put them in order from shortest to tallest.

**ORDERING WIDTH**

Collect plastic lids of varying circumferences. Children are to order them on the basis of width.

**ORDERING TEXTURES**

Collect varying grades of sandpaper. Children are to order them on the basis of texture, from the smoothest to the roughest.

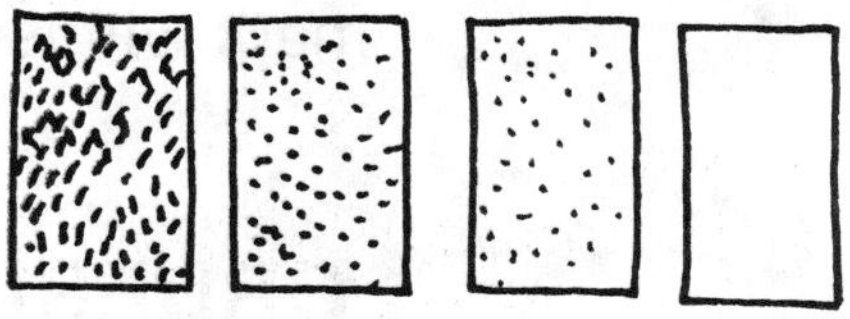

**ORDERING COLOR**

From a paint store collect paint samples of varying tones. Children are to order them from light to dark.

**ORDERING SOUND**

Collect empty Leggs eggs or plastic Easter eggs from a variety store. Inside each egg, place an object that will, when shaken, make a distinctly different sound or a sound louder than the other objects. Such objects can include a rock, large paper clip, lima bean, toothpick, rice, or cotton. Children are to shake each egg and order the eggs on the basis of sound, from the softest to the loudest.

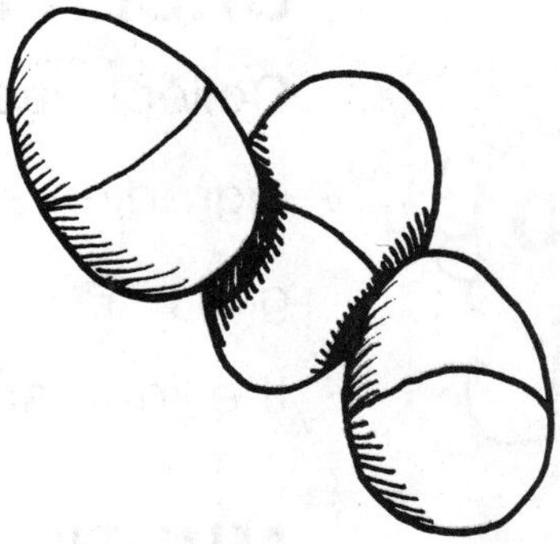

## 7 ORDERING WEIGHT

Find 5 identical boxes (5 manila envelopes can also be used). Place in each a substance that when picked up will feel different in weight from the other substances. Objects can include cotton, a sponge, a ruler, a magazine, or a bar of soap.

## 8 ORDERING VOLUME

Place 8 plastic cups inside each other for storage. Cups should all be the same size. With a permanent marking pen, make a mark on the outside of each cup. Each succeeding mark should be slightly higher than the mark on the previous cup. Children are to fill the cups to the mark with sand or water, and then order them from empty to full.

## 9 ORDERING NUMBER

On cardboard 4" × 4" cards, glue beans for the children to feel and count. Each card should have one more bean than the previous card. No written numbers should be visible. Children are to order the cards from 0 to 10.

## 10 ORDERING SMELL

Collect baby food jars. Place a small sample of each of the following ingredients in the bottom of the jar: flour, leather, sawdust, cloves, garlic. Punch several holes in the lids. Children are to order the jars from the lightest to the strongest smell.

## 11 MULTIPLE SERIATION

Make "packages" of varying sizes. "Wrap" each with wrapping paper. Make corresponding sized bows. Children are to match the package with the appropriate bow. Can they do it in reverse order, placing the smallest bow on the largest package, etc.?

# BLOCKS

A special math and reading contract for:

______________________________

Date: ______________________

Color each block as you complete the task.

# BLOCKS

## PURPOSE:

At this center, children will use activities involving writing, sorting, geometry, pattern, measurement, area, regrouping, beginning sound, letter recognition, and fine motor skills.

Blocks have been synonymous with early childhood education for years. Children spend long involved hours building creations. Why not capitalize on this motivation? Blocks can also be a tremendous tool for fostering language arts and mathematical concepts.

## BLOCKS:

Blocks can readily be purchased at teacher supply stores and at toy stores. They also can be easily acquired from scrap barrels in lumber yards. Covered milk cartons and shoe boxes can also be used. Effort should be made to provide a variety of different block shapes.

## ADDITIONAL MATERIALS:

* task cards covered with contact paper
* one contract for each child
* writing paper
* pencils
* one-inch colored block cubes
* classroom alphabet chart
* yardstick
* sand timer
* scissors
* paste
* construction paper
* measuring tape

*
Sorting loops can be easily made by tying yarn lengths in a knot.

# Sorting

1

Sort the blocks

into groups.

Can you sort them another way?
What was your reason for sorting the blocks the way you did?

# Story Time

2

Make a building with your blocks.

What did you build?

Write a story about your building.

# Shapes

3

Make these shapes with blocks.

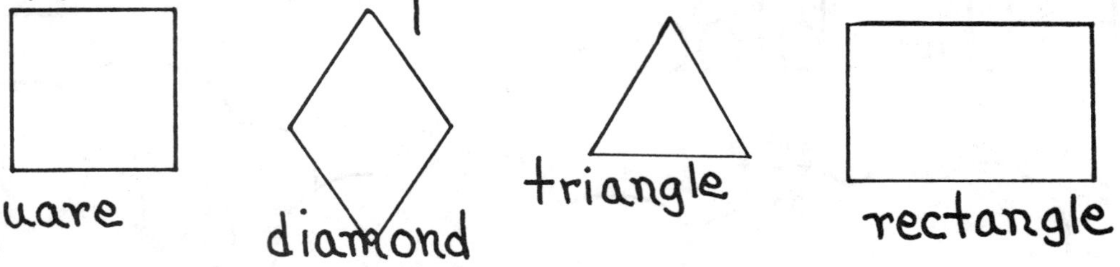


How many blocks did you need to use?

| | | | |
|---|---|---|---|
| square | ☐ | triangle | ☐ |
| diamond | ☐ | rectangle | ☐ |

# Patterns

4

Build these patterns:

| | | | | | | | |
|---|---|---|---|---|---|---|---|
| **1.** | red | blue | red | blue | red | **?** | **?** |
| **2.** | yellow | blue | red | yellow | blue | **?** | **?** |
| **3.** | blue | blue | red | blue | blue | **?** | **?** |

**4.** Build your own pattern.

# Sound Building

5

Build something that starts with these sounds:

**r** ____________ **b** ____________

**s** ____________ **t** ____________

Write the names of the things you built.

# Groupings

6

Put the blocks into groups with 10 blocks in each group.

I made ☐ groups of 10.

I had ☐ blocks left over.

# Block Letters

7

Look at the alphabet chart.

Aa Bb Cc Dd Ee Ff

How many letters can you build with the blocks?

Write the letters you make.

# Towers

8

You need:

yardstick

sand timer

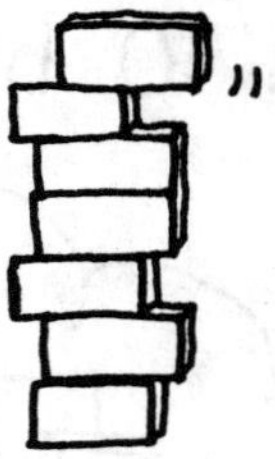

Build a block tower.

How high can you build it?
Measure it. It is ☐ inches high.

How high can you build a tower before the sand runs out?

Measure it. It is ☐ inches high.

## Roads

**9**

You need:

yardstick 

Make a road 6 inches long.
Make a road 12 inches long.
Make a road 24 inches long.
Make a road 36 inches long.

## Shape Art

**10**

You need:

scissors  paste 

 paper pencil

1. 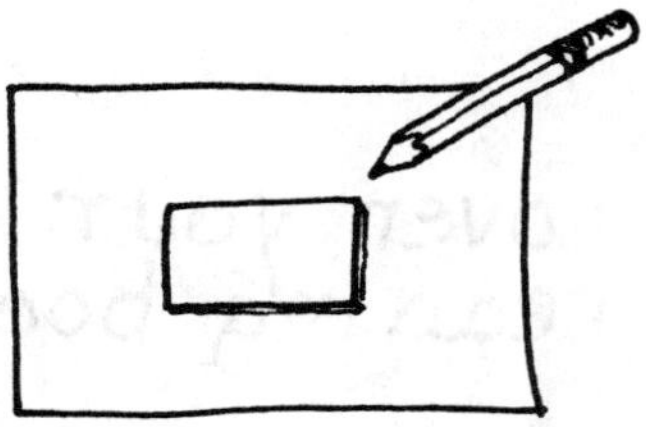 Trace around several different blocks on a piece of paper.

2.  Cut out the shapes.

3. 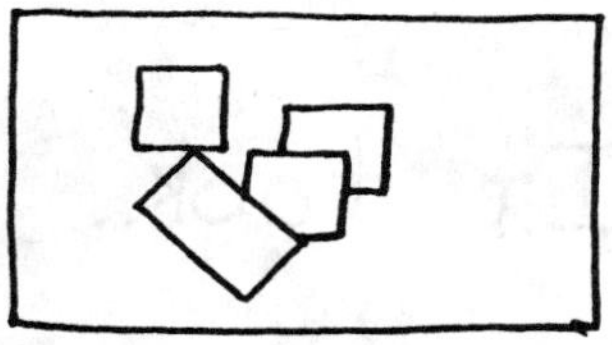 Paste down the shapes and make a picture. Add details with your pencil.

# Measure Me

**11**

**1.** Lie down.

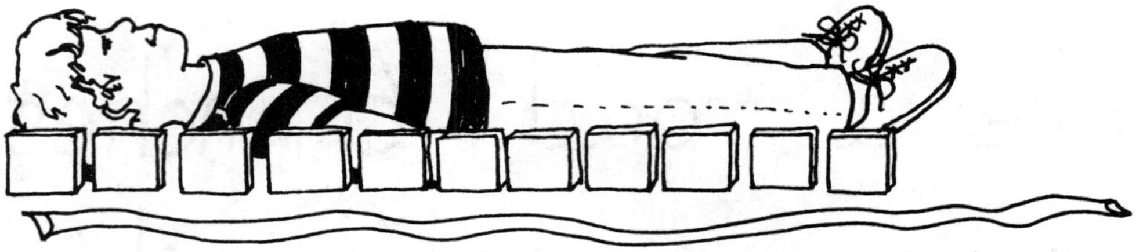

**2.** Line up blocks from your feet to your head in a straight line.

**3.**  Use a tape measure. How tall are you?

I am ☐ inches tall.

# Area

**12**

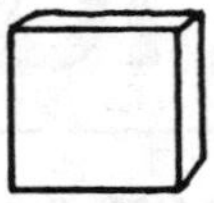 Use 1 inch cubes (blocks).

Guess, then measure.

How many blocks do you need to cover your reading book?

☐ I guessed. ☐ It took.

How many blocks do you need to cover the bottom of the inside of a shoebox?

☐ I guessed. ☐ It took.

# Graphing Center

**PURPOSE:** ① To develop "1-to-1" correspondence. ② To develop "greater than/ less than concepts. ③ To provide various counting experiences. ④ To familiarize children with graphs.

**MATERIALS:**

.... grocery store box decorated with graphs for the portable graphing center.
..... various colors of water colors, pens and pencils.
..... 2 sets of clothespins with each child's name.
..... coffee can sets filled and labeled with _ tangrams, plastic dinosaurs, scissors, colored beads, bottle caps.
..... graphing contract and worksheets for each child.
.... laminated tagboard graphs.

## PROCEDURE:

Graphing experiences will begin with actual objects plotted on tagboard graphs. These may be made from tagboard strips cut 6" × 28" and laminated. Other graphing experiences will be done with actual objects and the worksheets. Following each graph that the child does, a Graphing Investigation Worksheet will be filled out by the child. Children should explain each graph completed and state the relationship between the numbers: "there are more red dinosaurs than green dinosaurs....6 is greater than 4."

**1** * NOTE TO TEACHER Glue graph paper to tagboard and cut to 6"x 28" size. Fold, then write these directions.

Are there more girls or boys? Use the clothespins to show. Read the name on each clothespin. If it's a girl's name, clip it on the girl's side. If it's a boy's name, clip it on boy's side.

Fill out a graphing investigation form.

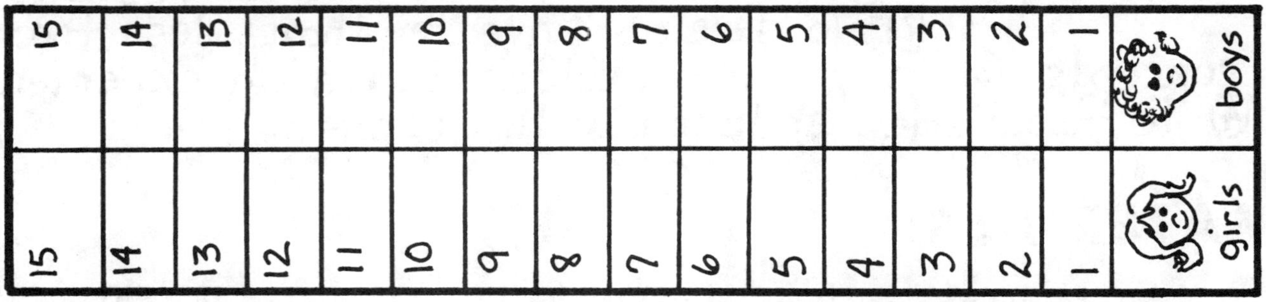


Graphing Investigation

Today I graphed ______

My discoveries:

There are ☐ girls.

There are ☐ boys

☐ is more than ☐

Children clip clothespins to graph to show the tally. They interpret the graph by filling out the worksheet.

## 2 SHOE TIES

Use name 

clothespins.

Look around room at your friends shoes. Are they tied or untied? Count how many of each. Place a clothespin by the correct number of each kind. Which is more? Fill out a graphing investigation form.

| | | | | | | | | | | | | | | | |
|---|---|---|---|---|---|---|---|---|---|---|---|---|---|---|---|
| 15 | 14 | 13 | 12 | 11 | 10 | 9 | 8 | 7 | 6 | 5 | 4 | 3 | 2 | 1 |  Don't Tie |
| 15 | 14 | 13 | 12 | 11 | 10 | 9 | 8 | 7 | 6 | 5 | 4 | 3 | 2 | 1 |  Tie |

## 3 LUNCHES

Use name 

clothespins.

Are there more people who bring their lunch from home than buy their lunch at school? Find out. Place clothespins. Complete form.

| | | | | | | | | | | | | | | | |
|---|---|---|---|---|---|---|---|---|---|---|---|---|---|---|---|
| 15 | 14 | 13 | 12 | 11 | 10 | 9 | 8 | 7 | 6 | 5 | 4 | 3 | 2 | 1 |  buy |
| 15 | 14 | 13 | 12 | 11 | 10 | 9 | 8 | 7 | 6 | 5 | 4 | 3 | 2 | 1 |  bring |

## 4 SCISSORS

Use the 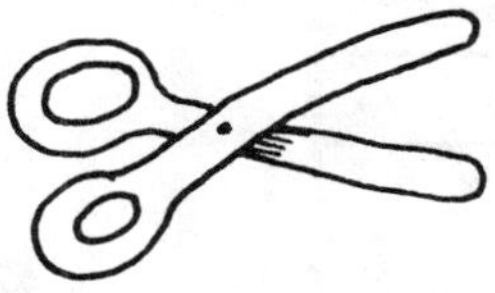 scissors.

Put a left-handed pair of green scissors in each square on the left-handed side of the chart. Begin with 1. Put a right-handed pair of scissors in each square on the right. Which side has more? Fill out an investigation form.

| | | | | | | | | | | | | | | | |
|---|---|---|---|---|---|---|---|---|---|---|---|---|---|---|---|
| 15 | 14 | 13 | 12 | 11 | 10 | 9 | 8 | 7 | 6 | 5 | 4 | 3 | 2 | 1 |  right |
| 15 | 14 | 13 | 12 | 11 | 10 | 9 | 8 | 7 | 6 | 5 | 4 | 3 | 2 | 1 |  left |

# WORKSHEETS: Place in activity envelopes.

5

6

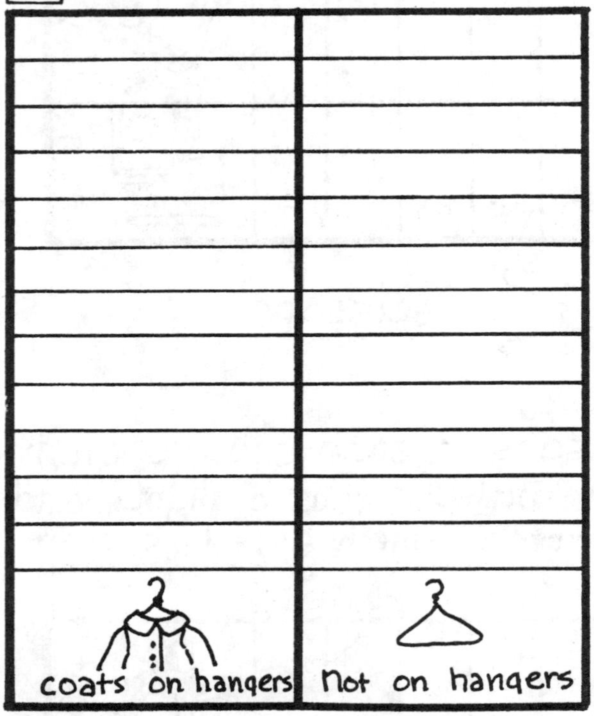


7

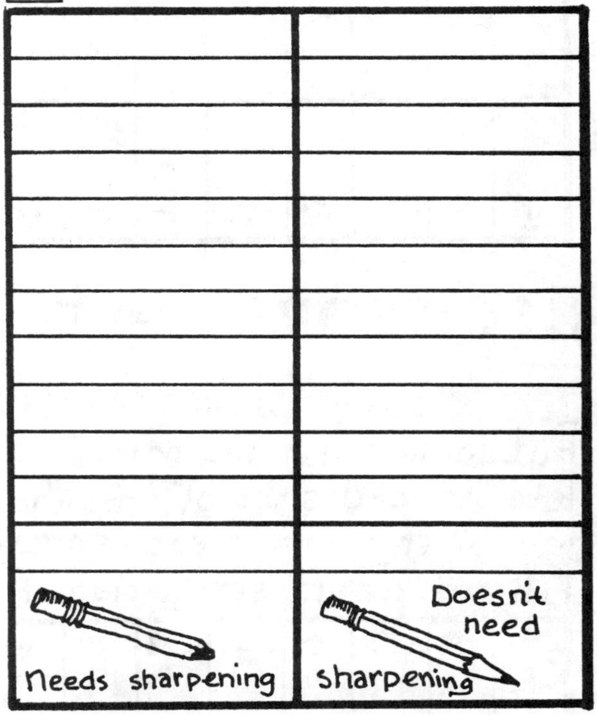


Students complete above worksheets using real objects from the "coffee can sets". Students color in each number box after filling out investigation sheet.

## 8 DINOSAUR GRAPHING

You need:  Dinosaur Can

Find all the dinosaurs that are the same color. Plot them on the graph by shading. Complete an investigation form.

| | | | | | | | | | | | | |
|---|---|---|---|---|---|---|---|---|---|---|---|---|
| | | | | | | | | | | | | blue |
| | | | | | | | | | | | | red |
| | | | | | | | | | | | | yellow |
| 12 | 11 | 10 | 9 | 8 | 7 | 6 | 5 | 4 | 3 | 2 | 1 | green |

## 9 BOTTLE CAP GRAPHING

You need:  Bottle Caps Can

Find all the bottle caps like the ones below. Discover how many of each cap there are. Plot the results on the graph. Complete an investigation form.

| | | | | | | | | | | | | |
|---|---|---|---|---|---|---|---|---|---|---|---|---|
| | | | | | | | | | | | | Pepsi |
| | | | | | | | | | | | | Coke |
| | | | | | | | | | | | | 7-up |
| 12 | 11 | 10 | 9 | 8 | 7 | 6 | 5 | 4 | 3 | 2 | 1 | Like |

## 10 BEAD STRINGING

You need:  Bead can

STRING THE BEADS - Write the number of each bead in each box. ☐

☐ red ☐ blue ☐ yellow ☐ green

Tie a real bead with a shoelace to each box. Complete a form.

# WORKSHEETS: Place in activity folder.

| 11 | HAIR COLOR | | |
|---|---|---|---|
| 11 | | | |
| 10 | | | |
| 9 | | | |
| 8 | | | |
| 7 | | | |
| 6 | | | |
| 5 | | | |
| 4 | | | |
| 3 | | | |
| 2 | | | |
| 1 | | | |
| Brown | Yellow | Black | Red |

| 12 | TANGRAMS | | |
|---|---|---|---|
| 11 | | | |
| 10 | | | |
| 9 | | | |
| 8 | | | |
| 7 | | | |
| 6 | | | |
| 5 | | | |
| 4 | | | |
| 3 | | | |
| 2 | | | |
| 1 | | | |
| △ orange | △ green | △ blue | △ purple |

## Graphing Investigation

Today I graphed ________ (picture)

MY DISCOVERIES!

There are ☐ (number) ________ (word)

There are ☐ (number) ________ (word)

☐ is more than ☐

by ________

Name ________

## Graphing Investigation

Today I graphed ☐

I discovered:

There are ☐ ________

There are ☐ ________

There are ☐ ________

There are ☐ ________

☐ is the most ☐ is the least

* NOTE TO TEACHER You may wish to increase the size of each of these worksheets before duplicating

# Subtraction

## PURPOSE:

To develop the numeric skills of subtraction.

## MATERIALS:

* grocery box covered with contact paper and decorated with hearts.
* stationery envelopes the size of the box to hold materials and activity cards.
* subtraction contract for each child.

* watercolor pens to write on activity cards.
* activity cards written on tagboard and laminated.
* damp sponge pieces for "erasers."

NOTE: This easily can be converted to an "addition box" by changing each problem.

## ACTIVITY CARDS:

1 MATERIALS NEEDED:
popsicle sticks, library pockets, directions written on envelope

| | | | |
|---|---|---|---|
| You need: sticks, envelopes (4-2) | A. (4-2) Put in 4 sticks | B. (4-2) Take out 2 sticks. | Count how many sticks are left. |

* NOTE TO TEACHER Make several subtraction problems on library pockets. Put them inside the activity envelope.

## 2 Paper Clips

You need:

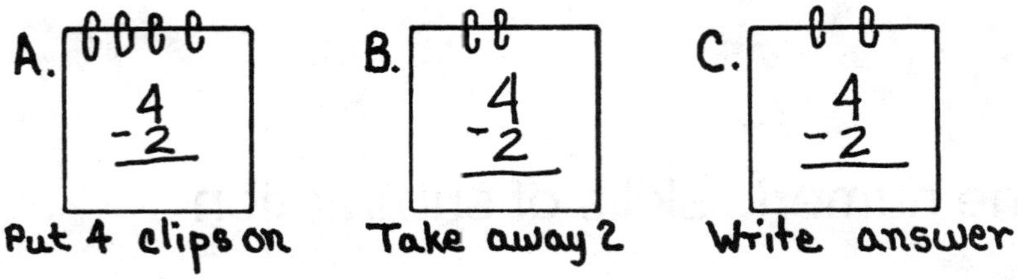


Make several subtraction cards similar to those shown above. Use problems from your basic textbook. Laminate each card so students can write on them.

## 3 Erase It!

You need:

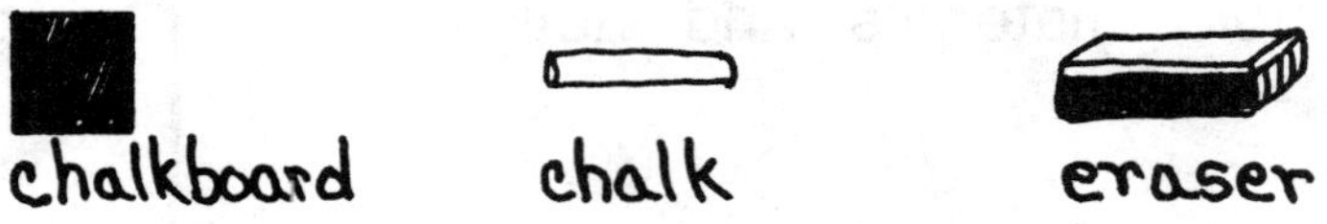


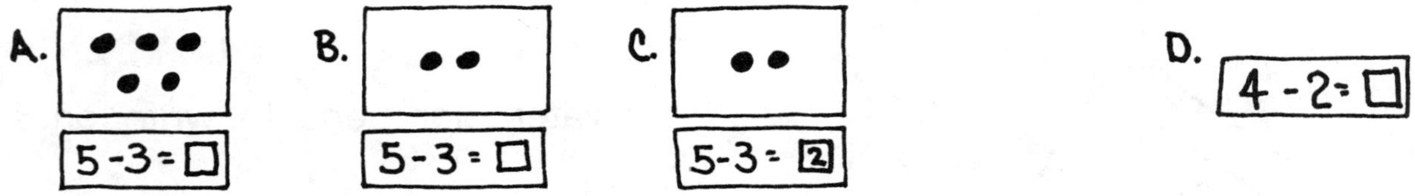


A. Make 5 dots on the chalkboard.
B. Erase 3 dots.
C. Write how many are left.
D. Pick another card.

Use 2"x4" pieces of tagboard and make several subtraction cards. Laminate each card so students can write on them.

## 4 Bead Stringing!

You need:

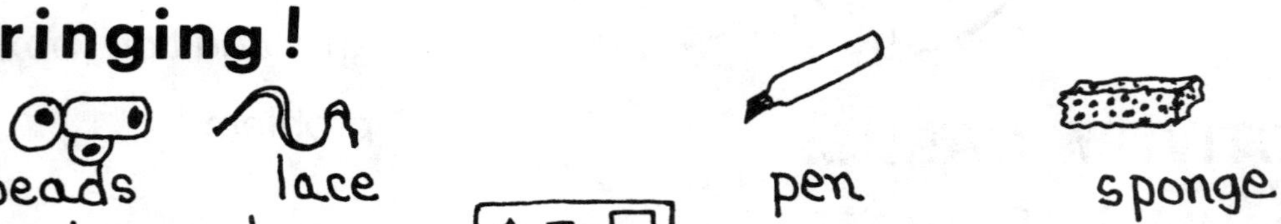


Look at each card ........ 4-3=☐

A. String 4 beads
B. Take off 3 beads

C. How many beads are left?

Write your answer with the pen. Do all cards.

* NOTE TO TEACHER Make several cards as in activity #3.

## (5) Zoo Subtraction!

You need:

cards pen can "zoo" sponge

See how many animals you can save from the lion.

Look at each card. Solve it.

A. 3-2=□ Put 3 animals in the cage.

B. 3-2=□ Take 2 animals out of the cage.

C. 3-2=1 How many animals were saved from the lion? Write your answer.

D. Do the rest of the cards.

*NOTE TO THE TEACHER An empty strawberry basket turned upside down makes an excellent "zoo". Animals for the zoo can be purchased at most variety stores. Make several 2" x 4" subtraction cards from tagboard. Laminate each card.

## (6) Geoboard Subtraction

You need:

cards geoboard rubber bands pens sponge

Look at each card...... 4-2=□

A. Put a rubber band around four nails.

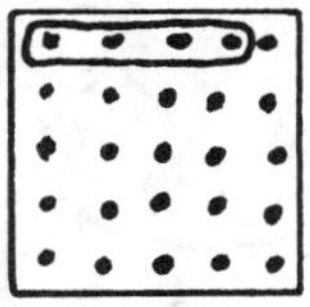

B.

Take the rubber band off two nails.

C. 4-2=2 How many are left?

*NOTE TO TEACHER

A geoboard can easily be made by nailing 25 nails (in rows of 5) into an 8" x 8" scrap of wood. Make several subtraction cards.

## 7 Water Game

You need:

sink

5 cups

water color pen

A.  Fill a small tub with water.

B. Look at each card. 5-3=☐

C.  Fill 5 cups with water.

D.  Empty 3 cups.

E. How many cup are still full? Write your answer. 5-3=2

F. Solve the other cards. Keep using the same tub of water.

* NOTE TO TEACHER You may wish to use sand rather than water for this game. Make several subtraction cards and laminate them.

## 8 Button Game

You need: 3-2=☐

coat

button can

pen

sponge

A. Look carefully at the card. 3-2=☐

B. You have 3 buttons on your coat. 

C. You lose 2 buttons. 

D. How many buttons are left on your coat? Write 3-2=1 the answer.

* NOTE TO TEACHER Make a coat pattern from cardboard. Place it in the activity envelope. Fill a can with old buttons. Make and laminate several cards.

## 9 Squirrel & Acorns

You need:

A. Look carefully at the card: 5-2=☐

B. Put 5  acorns on the tree.

C.  A squirrel came along and ate 2 acorns.

D.  How many are left? 5-2=3 Write your answer.

*NOTE TO TEACHER Make a tree pattern from cardboard. Place pattern in activity folder. Fill a coffee can with acorns. Label the can. Make and laminate several subtraction cards.

## 10 Caves

You need:

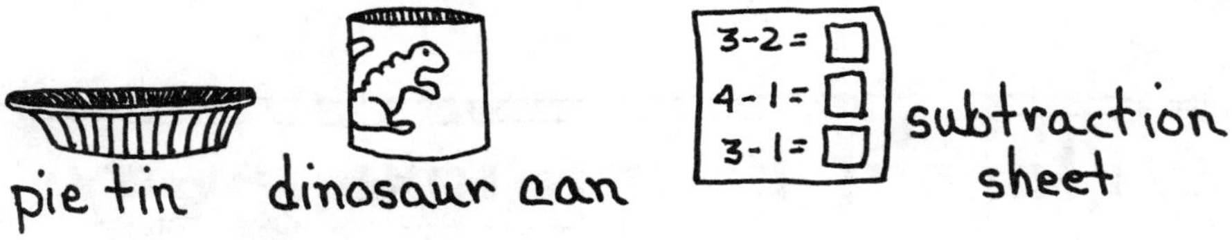


Help hide the dinosaurs in the cave from the meat-eating dinosaur. Look carefully at the first problem.

A. 3-2=☐ Put 3 dinosaurs under  the cave.

B. 3-2=☐ Take 2 dinosaurs out. 

C. How many dinosaurs are left? 3-2=1 Write your answer.

*NOTE TO TEACHER: Make and laminate several subtraction cards. Plastic dinosaurs can be purchased at most variety stores. Place them in a coffee can.

## (11) Jack & the Beanstalk

You need:

subtraction sheet, bean can, beanstalk

Help Jack climb the beanstalk. Look carefully at the card.

A. [5-3= □] Jack had 5 beans. Put them on the beanstalk.

B. [5-3= □] Jack lost 3 beans.

C. [5-3= 2] How many are left? Write the number of beans that Jack has left.

*NOTE TO TEACHER: Make and laminate a subtraction sheet. Fill a coffee can with dried lima beans. On a piece of tagboard, draw a green beanstalk. Cut leaves from green construction paper.

## (12) Flannel Board Take Away

You need:

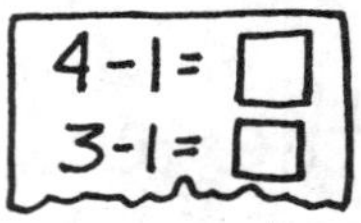


subtraction sheet

flannel board

flannel board figures

Look carefully at the first problem.

A. [4-3= □] Put 4 figures on the flannel board.

B [4-3= □] Take 3 of the figures away.

C. How many figures are left? Write your answer. [4-3= 1]

*NOTE TO TEACHER: On cardboard make and laminate a subtraction sheet. Cover a piece of cardboard with flannel. Make several small shapes of flannel.

# Volume

## PURPOSE:

To experience conservation of liquid through active manipulation of volume. To discover the relationship of cups, pints and quarts through manipulation of containers. To estimate size relationships. To develop hand-eye coordination.

## MATERIALS:

* grocery box covered with contact paper and decorated with pictures of cups and containers to store the "portable center."
* volume contract for each child.
* cardboard cut in lengths to fit the box.
* activity cards may be made directly on the cardboard (or heavy tagboard).
* containers in assorted sizes, including cup, pint, quart, ½ cup, ⅓ cup, ¼ cup, funnel, teaspoons and tablespoons. Label the containers with a marking pen.
* large tub, pail or plastic laundry bin to do the tasks in.

* sponges!
* watercolor pens.
* different sized containers, labeled A, B, C, D, E.
* 10 glasses of the same size, with a marking pen horizontal line across each glass, gradually increasing in height on each succeeding glass.

## ACTIVITY CARDS:

Copy each activity on a 9" × 12" tagboard sheet. Laminate the boards so that children can write directly on the sheet with a watercolor pen.

## 1 FILL IT UP!

A. Place in a line the containers that have rubber bands on them.

B. Fill the quart pitcher with water. Look carefully at the small containers. Fill each to the line.

## 2 WHICH TAKES LONGER?

You need:

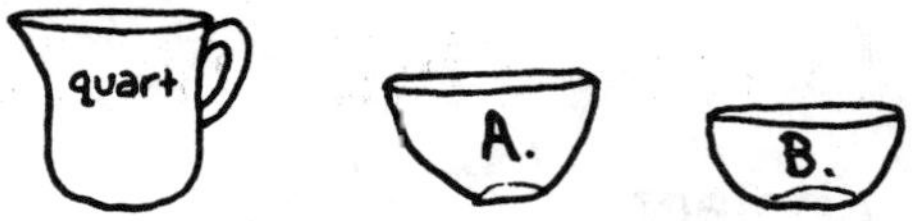


2 containers each a different size. You choose.

A. Fill the first container with water. Pour the water into the pitcher. How many containers of water does it take to fill the pitcher? Write the number. ☐

B. Fill the second container with water. Pour the water into the pitcher. Write down how many containers it takes to fill the pitcher. ☐

C. Which took longer "A" or "B"? Why?

## 3 QUART FILLING

You need:

A. Fill the cup with water. Pour it into the quart pitcher.

B. How many cups of water fill the quart? Write your answer. ☐

## 4 ORDERING GAME!

You need:

10 glasses

A. Carefully fill each glass to the line.

B. Put the glasses in order from the least amount of water to the most.

## 5 WHICH HOLDS THE MOST?

You need:

cup

_____ _____ _____ _____

A. How many cups of water will fill each container?

Write your guess on the lines above.

B. Check and see if you guessed right. How many cups does it take? Write the answers below.

A. _____ B. _____ C. _____ D. _____

## 6 LIQUID MEASUREMENT

You need:

A. Which container is the biggest?

How will you find out?

B. Put the containers in a line, smallest to biggest.

_____ _____ _____ _____ _____

## 7 QUARTS & PINTS

You need: cup, pint, quart

1 quart = ☐ cups.

1 pint = ☐ cups.

1 quart = ☐ pints.

2 pints = ☐ quarts.

## 8 CUPS & SPOONS

You need: cup, tablespoons

1 cup = ☐ tablespoons

½ cup = ☐ table spoons

¼ cup = ☐ tablespoons

## 9 CUPS & PINTS

You need: cup, ½, ¼, 1 pint

1 cup = ☐ ¼ cups

1 cup = ☐ ½ cups

½ cup = ☐ ¼ cups

1 pint = ☐ cups

1 pint = ☐ ½ cups

LISTENING

**PURPOSE:**

To develop an appreciation of a variety of tempos. To develop an awareness of rhythm and pitch.

# MATERIALS NEEDED:

1 Record player, headphones, listening post
1 contract for each child
Envelope with pictures of different instruments
Writing worksheet — 1 for each child

2 Metronome
"Metronome" worksheet — 1 for each child

3 3 different records marked "1", "2", "3" on the record jackets. These records should represent 3 different tempos (fast, slow, fast and slow). Box marked "Rating Box."
"Rate that Tune" worksheet — 1 for each child

4 Any record which has an accompanying song sheet with the lyrics written out.
"Song Report" worksheet — 1 for each child

5 Instrument Chart posted on the board.
Children may help bring the following materials from home to make the instruments:

| | |
|---|---|
| shoe boxes | oatmeal cartons |
| rubber bands | chicken barrels |
| paper plates | sticks cut 8" × ½" |
| pebbles, rice, beans | bottle caps |
| wood blocks | nails |
| sandpaper | hammer |
| glue/thumbtacks | combs |
| Decorating Materials: | |
| scissors | sequins |
| yarn | glitter |
| large pieces of drawing paper | construction paper |
| crayons | paste |

6 Peter and the Wolf

## WRITING TIME

1. Look at the instrument cards.

   Choose one.

2. 

   Pretend you are an instrument that comes to life. Write a story. Where do you live? Who are your friends? What is a day in your life like? How do you feel?

## METRONOMES

1. Music can be fast

   or slow.

   Metronomes help musicians stay on the beat.

2. Turn on the metronome.

   Listen carefully. Stamp your foot to the beat.

3. Take music paper number 2. Turn metronone to 60. Color to the beat on the slow side.

4. Turn metronome to 120. Color to fast side.

## RATE THAT TUNE

1. Listen carefully to records 1, 2, and 3.

2. As you listen to each record fill out the special rating sheet.

3. Put your rating sheets in rating box.

## SONG REPORT

1. Listen carefully to RECORD 4.

2. Read along with the song sheet.

3. Draw a picture showing what the song was about. Write a sentence about picture.

## MAKE AN INSTRUMENT

5

Choose 1 instrument to make.

Read the instrument chart for help.

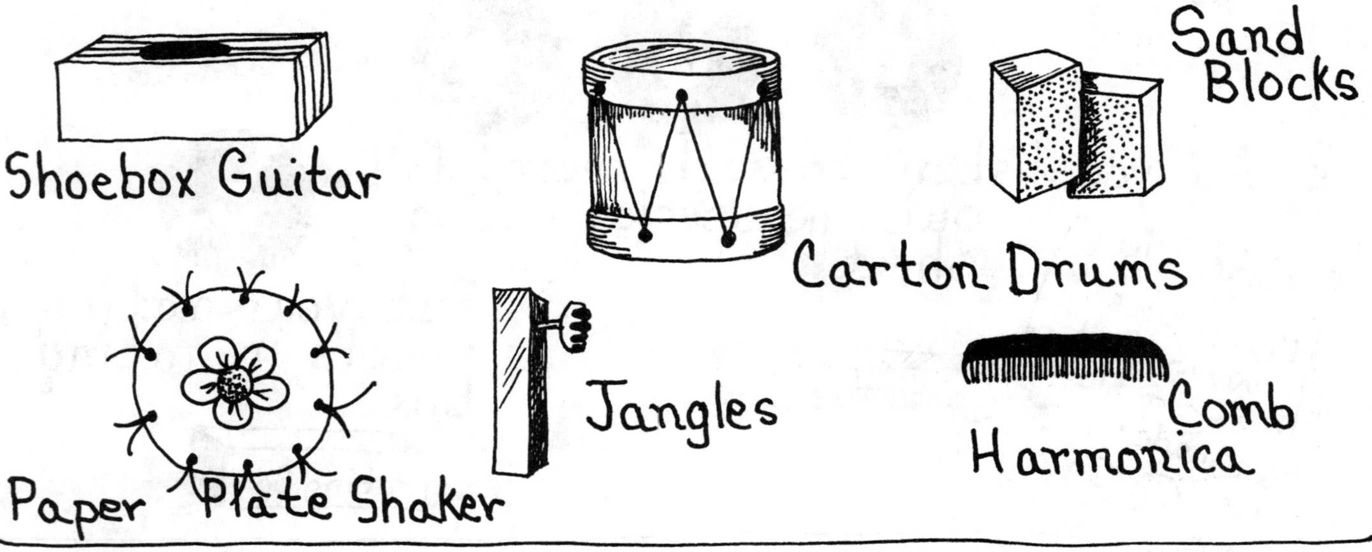


## COLOR TO MUSIC

6

1. Music can show different feelings. Listen carefully to the music - PETER and the WOLF.

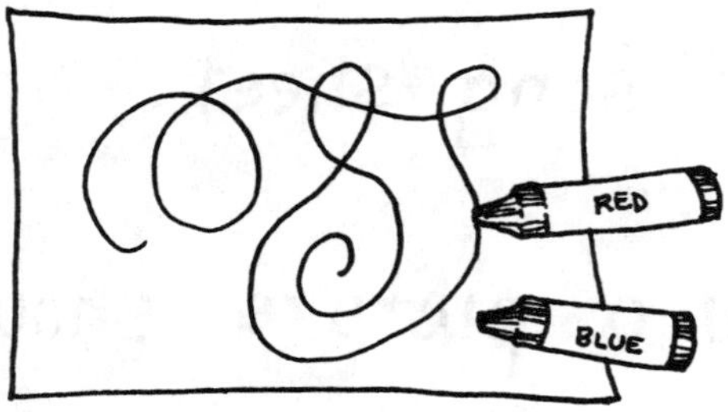


2. Color to the music. Go fast when the music is fast and slow when music is slow.

You need:

crayons

paper

# WORKSHEETS

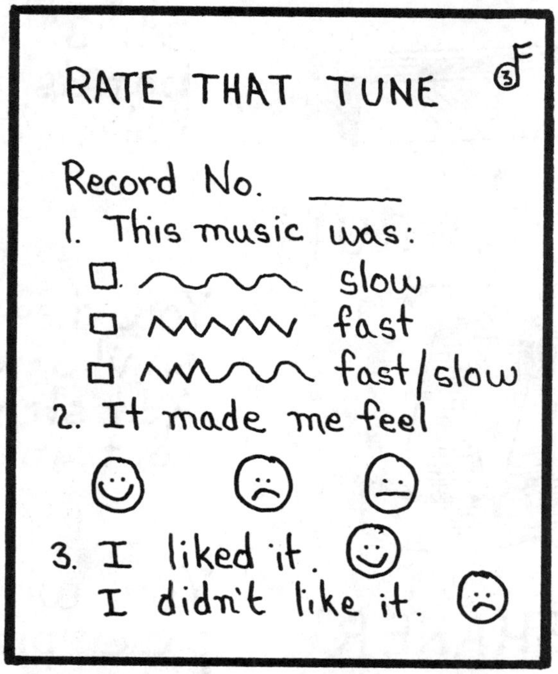


* NOTE TO TEACHER You will need to make master copies and duplicate the four worksheets on this page.

The instrument chart on the next page is ready to duplicate and use.

# INSTRUMENT CHART

## GUITAR

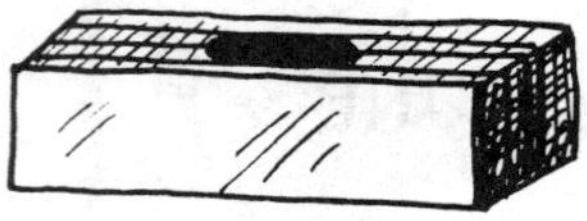

You need a shoebox. Cut a hole about 3"x 3" in the top lid. Wrap 5 rubber bands around the box and over the hole. Decorate the box with paint.

## DRUM

You need an empty oatmeal box or similar round carton. Paint and decorate. Add string. Be sure to keep top on the container.

## SHAKER

You will need two paper plates. Staple, lace or glue the plates together – BUT – before you do, fill the inside with rice or dried beans. Add yarn fringe. Decorate with magic marker.

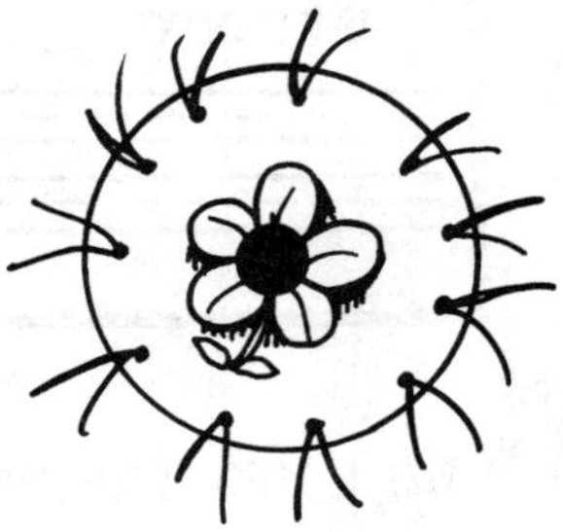

## JANGLES

You will need a stick about 8"x ½". Flatten four bottle caps with a hammer. Attach two bottle caps, with a nail, to each stick. You may wish to paint the wood.

## SAND BLOCKS

You will need 2 blocks of wood about 4" square. Paint the wood if you wish. Glue or tack sandpaper to 1 side of each wood block.

## COMB HARMONICA

Very simple to make. Wrap wax paper around comb. Use rubber band to hold.

# MUSIC CONTRACT

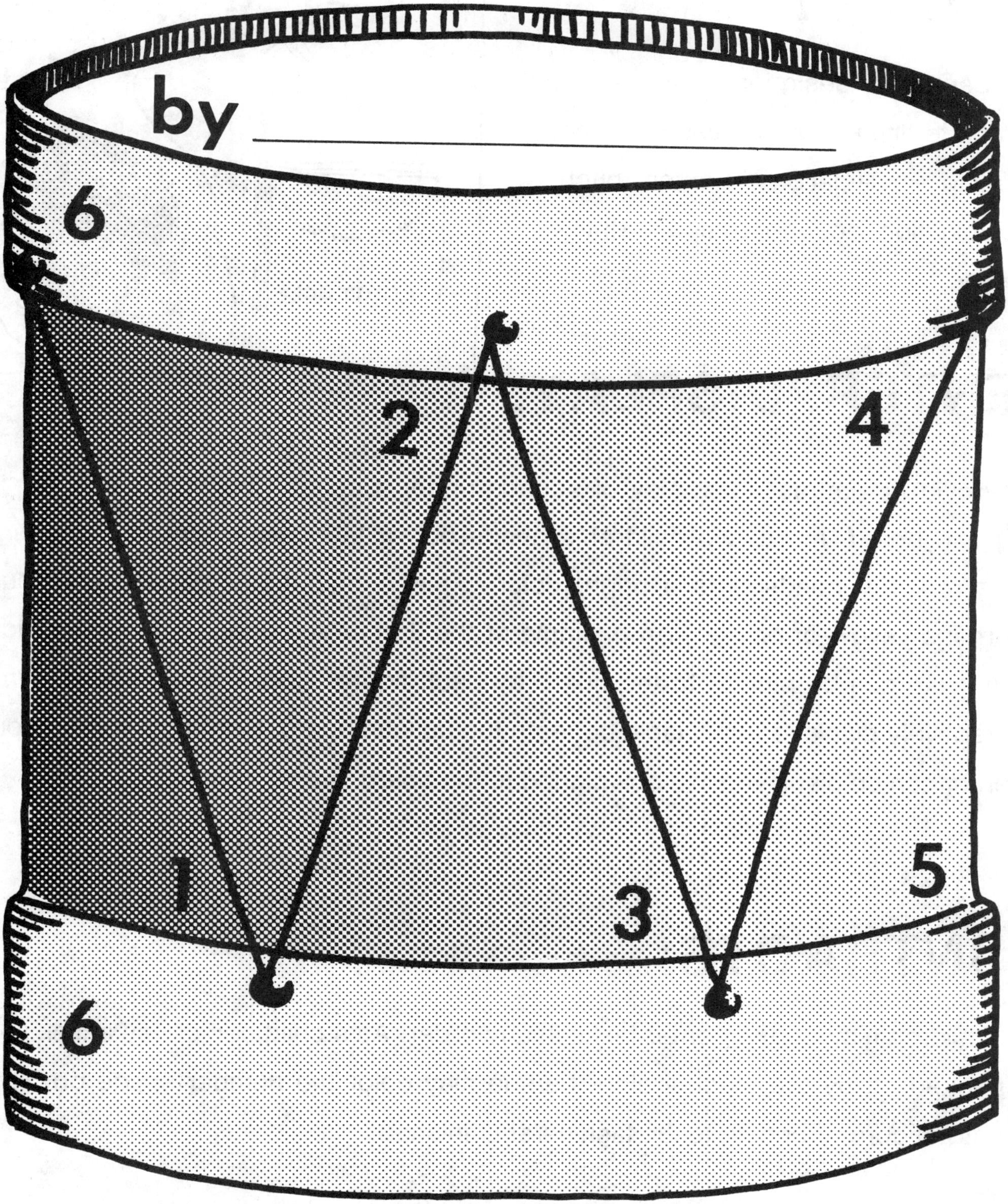


Color each number space as you complete the task with the same number.

# SOUND

## PURPOSE:

The center is designed to introduce children to different properties of sound, including amplification, vibration, pitch, discrimination, sequence, and attentive listening.

## CENTER DISPLAY:

Provide an attractive display of sounds under a colorful bulletin board. For the bulletin board, make two children's heads out of tagboard. Paint or color in the features. Pin heads onto a bright colored piece of butcher paper background, perhaps yellow or orange. An example of the tin can telephones that the children will make can be pinned to the board by each figure. Books about sound can be attractively displayed on a table beneath the bulletin board. Contracts for the sound center can be displayed in a box pinned to the board.

## CONTRACTS:

Children may do the center tasks in any order. As a child completes a task and is checked off by the teacher/aide, he/she may color the number space on his/her contract corresponding to the task he/she finished.

Older children may write their discoveries for each task in a separate "Sound Book" made with a construction paper cover with writing paper stapled inside.

# MATERIALS:

At the center provide:

10 laminated task cards

pencils, crayons, scissors

writing and drawing paper

contract for each child

1 * Each child can be responsible for bringing two tin cans from home. The top must be completely cut out. A note can be sent home the week before, alerting parents to the project. Make one sample for the bulletin board display.

* Cord

* Hammer and nail to make the hole in the bottom of each can.

2 * Writing paper, pencils, crayons.

3 * Make the experiment ahead of time. Cut a piece of string about 3 feet long. Tie a spoon in the middle of the string. Display a fork and larger metal spoons, plus another 3 foot long string on the table for further experiments.

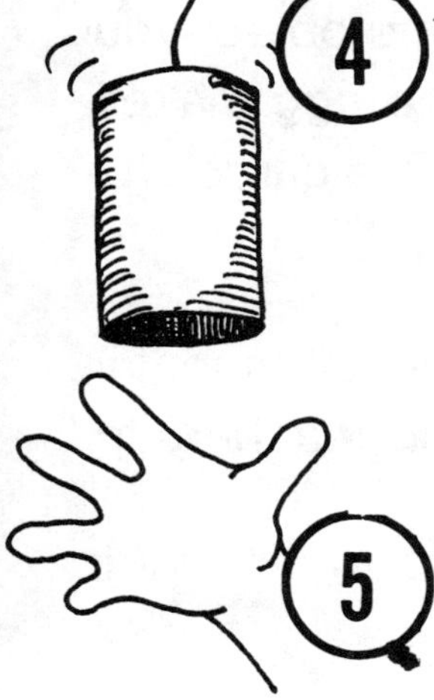

4 * Five glasses of the same size are needed. Number each glass from 1 to 5 with a marking pen. Fill each glass with water so that each succeeding glass contains slightly more water than the preceding one. Place the glasses in a cardboard box lid to soak up any spilled water. A metal spoon is needed. The song the children will play is "Mary Had a Little Lamb." Encourage children to create their own tunes.

5 * Provide enough paper straws for each child. Encourage children to find other instruments that make high and low sounds.

6 Display a large selection of classroom instruments. Drums, cymbals, bells, sand blocks, rhythm sticks, triangles, jangles, tambourines, etc., are great for a start. Encourage children to experiment with the instruments and create rhythm patterns.

7 A paper cup can provide a discovery method for the process of sound amplification. Cut out the bottom of the cup. Children can then use the cup as a crude stethoscope. Provide a sandtimer.

8 Save the containers from Leggs stockings or plastic Easter eggs (available in most variety stores). Inside two eggs put the same object to make "Sound Pairs." Make about five egg-sound pairs. The sounds must be similar so the chilren can try to distinguish one from another. Some ideas can include: cotton, rice, beans, tacks or nails, large rocks, jingle bells.

Make five "pair boards" corresponding to the number of pairs you make. Make the boards from cardboard. Draw two circles on each board where the children can place the two pairs. Put all the eggs and boards in a shoe box with the number "1" written on it.

9 You need five Legg Eggs or large plastic Easter eggs. Inside each egg place a different object such as: cotton, tack, paperclip, rock, toothpick. On a cardboard card paste a sample of the same object you placed inside the egg. The child will match the sound the egg makes with the object. You will need five cardboard cards. Place the cards and eggs in a shoe box with the number "2" on it.

10 You will need a Buzzer Board. They are available from Developmental Learning Materials. But, check first, the special education teachers in your school may already have one.

# SOUND CONTRACT

Color the picture as you finish the task. What sounds does it make?

Name ______________

# TIN CAN TELEPHONE (1)

You need:

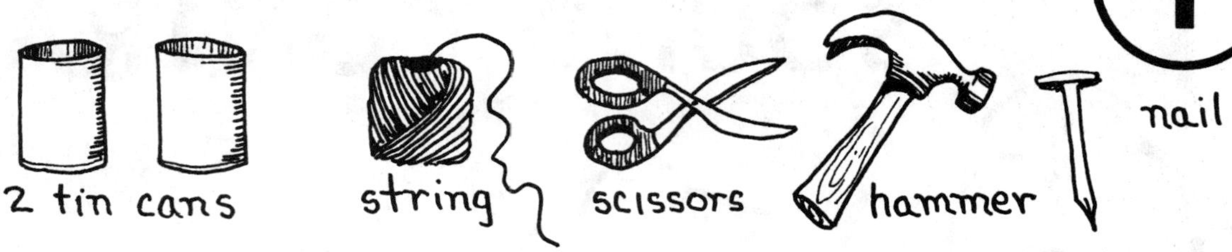

1. Make a hole in the bottom of the two tin cans you brought from home.
2. Cut a piece of string as long as the teacher's desk.
3. Pull the string inside each hole. Knot it on the inside of each can. You and a friend practice speaking and listening. How does it work?

# CLASSROOM SOUNDS (2)

1. Sit at your desk. Close your eyes. Listen carefully to all the sounds around you.
2. Open your eyes and draw a picture of the sounds you heard.

3. Write the name by each sound you draw.

# VIBRATIONS

## 3

You need:  Spoon tied to a string

1.  Gently tap the spoon against the table.

2. Put the string up to your ears and listen to the vibrations. The vibrations from the spoon are traveling along the string.

3. Try the same thing with a fork and with a larger spoon. Is the sound the same?

# MUSICAL GLASSES

## 4

Listen carefully to the different sounds in the glasses by gently tapping the spoon on the glass.

Can you play this song?

3 → 2 → 1 → 2 → 3 → 3 → 3 → 2 → 2 → 2 → 3

5 → 5 → 3 → 2 → 1 → 2 → 3 → 3 → 3 → 3 → 2

2 → 3 → 2 → 1

What is the song?

# HIGH & LOW

## 5

You need  straw 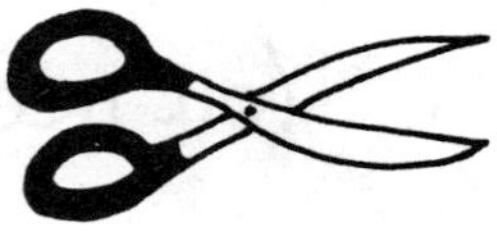 scissors

1. Flatten the last ½ inch of one end of the straw.
2.  Cut the flattened end as shown.
3.  Put the flattened end between your teeth and blow. Practice!
4. Now cut off a  bit of the straw. Blow again. Cut off more. Blow again. What is happening to the sound?

# INSTRUMENTS

## 6

1. Look at all of the instruments.

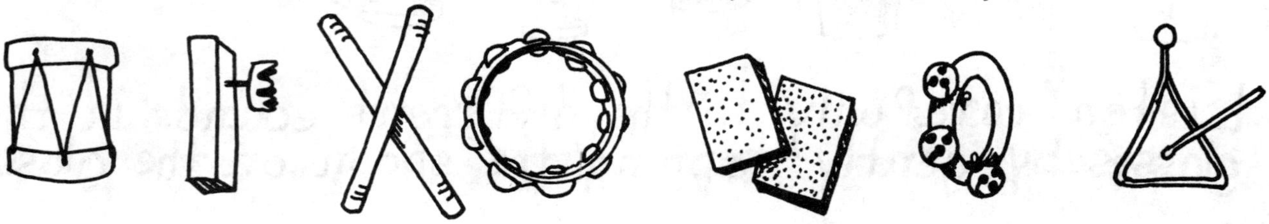

2. Choose 5 different instruments.
   Practice playing them.
   Do they sound alike?
   Put them in order, softest to loudest.

# 7 STETHOSCOPE

You need: A friend,

a paper cup

& a timer.

Place the small end of the cup to your ear and the big part of the cup to your friend's heart. What do you hear?

Change places. Let your friend have a turn.

How many beats do you hear before the sand runs out?

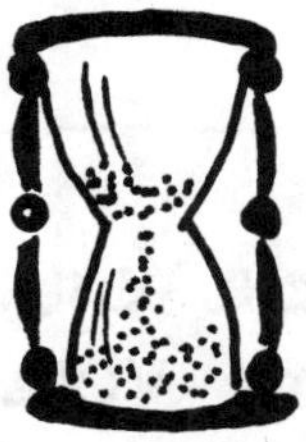

# SOUND PAIRS 8

1. Take

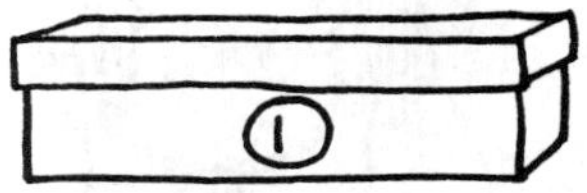

2. Shake each egg and listen carefully. Can you find the eggs that sound alike?

When you find each pair put them "side-

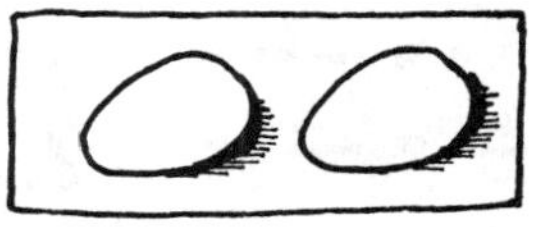

by-side" on the pair board.

# MATCH THE SOUND 9

You need:

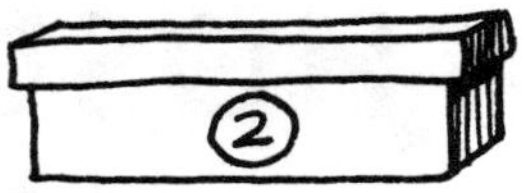


1. Listen carefully to each egg. What do you think is inside?

2. Match the egg to the correct picture card. Can you identify the cotton?

# MORSE CODE 10

Try sending letters! Try sending words!

| | | | | | | | |
|---|---|---|---|---|---|---|---|
| A | •— | B | —••• | C | —•—• | | |
| E | • | F | ••—• | G | ——• | D | —•• |
| I | •• | J | •——— | K | —•— | H | •••• |
| M | —— | N | —• | O | ——— | L | •—•• |
| Q | ——•— | R | •—• | S | ••• | P | •——• |
| U | ••— | V | •••— | W | •—— | T | — |
| Y | —•—— | Z | ——•• | | | X | —••— |

Practice sending the Morse Code on the buzzer board. Can your friend guess what letters you are sending?

# OBSERVATION SHEET

SCIENTIST ______________________________

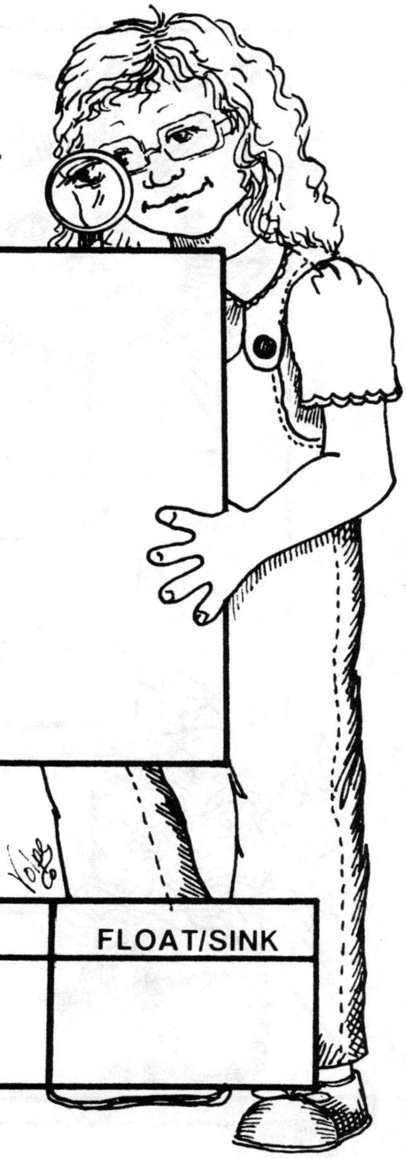

Picture of Object I Observed

## EXPERIMENTS

| ROLL | BOUNCE | SLIDE | SQUEEZE | FLOAT/SINK |
|---|---|---|---|---|
| | | | | |

## DESCRIBE THE OBJECT

At this center students will have the opportunity to become familiar with four conservation experiences.

**fire prevention** **water conservation**
**recycling processes** **ground beautification**

# MATERIALS

* paper bag per child
* 18" × 11" paper per child
* large box to store cans from home
* ditto page per child to write letter to janitor
* construction paper book filled with blank writing paper titled, "Save Water."

A special group lesson may precede the center, reminding children about the letter formation. When all the letters have been finished, invite the school janitor to your room and present the letters to him in a specially bound book.

A special class trip to the Recycling Center nearest your school might be worthwhile.

Awards for SPECIAL CONSERVA—TIONISTS can be presented at the end of the unit.

# CONSERVATION CONTRACT

BY ______________________________

Make a fire prevention poster for Smokey the Bear. Show him how you'll prevent fires.

Decorate a paper bag. Fill it with trash you collect from the school grounds.

Write a letter to your school janitor. Tell him how you will help him to keep the school building clean.

Find out where your home water meter is located. This month my family used ☐ cubic feet of water. Next month we will try to use only ☐ cu. ft.

On a page in the class Conservation Book, list ways your family could save water. Draw pictures.

From home bring cans that can be recycled.

I brought ☐ cans from home.

I counted ☐ cans in the box.

# WEATHER

## PURPOSE

To familiarize children with "weather vocabulary," evaporation, and heat expansion.

To experiment with thermometers and change in weather.

To strengthen observation skills.

## MATERIALS

* One weather contract for each child.
* One weather chart worksheet for each child.
* Display table for the study about weather.
  —Pictures depicting different kinds of weather.
  —Library books about weather.
  —Cloud or sun shaped books for optional stories.
  —Sign up sheet for weather forecast reports.
  —As many thermometers as available.

1 Weather Chart Worksheet for each child, pencils.

2 At least 2 thermometers, (any extra would be very beneficial), 2 coffee cans - 1 covered with black construction paper, 1 covered with white construction paper.

—Teach children how to read a thermometer.

—Encourage children to find out why the black can became hotter. What color clothes should be worn in hot weather?

3 Each day, as part of the class opening, include the weather report. These can be done by children bringing in their news bulletins.

4 2 thermometers, pencils. 1 thermometer should be placed near a sunny window, the other in a shady place. Encourage children to explain why one thermometer was much hotter.

5 thermometer, pencil

6 2 glasses for each child (can be brought from home), marking pen, ½ cup measuring device, water.

# WEATHER

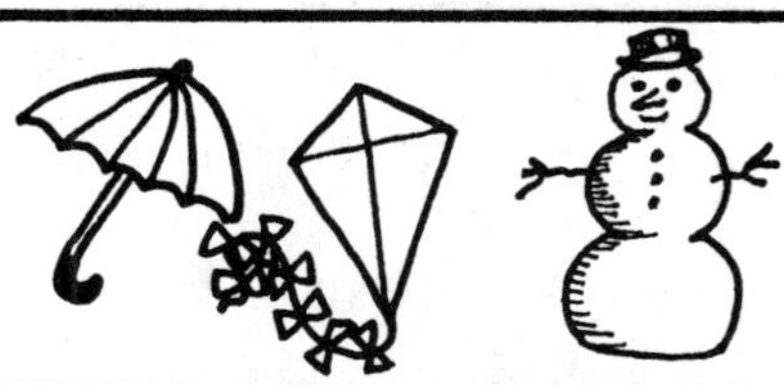

Name

**1**

Use the weather chart.
Each day look carefully outside.

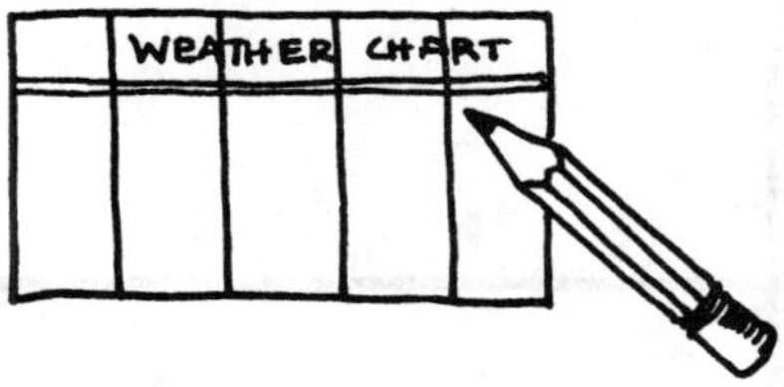


Draw a picture of the weather.
Write how the weather looks.

**2**

<u>Hot</u> <u>and</u> <u>Cold</u> You need..........

Put a thermometer in each can. Put both cans outside for 1 hour. Look at the temperatures. Which is hotter? Why?

**3**

<u>BE A WEATHERPERSON!</u>

You need.....

Look at the newspaper. Find the weather forecast. Cut it out. Bring it to school.
During "weather time", tell the weather forecast. Was it correct?

**4**

TEMPERATURE!

2  You need

At the same time....
....put a thermometer outside for 1/2 hour.
.....put a thermometer inside the classroom for 1/2 hour.
What is the temperature? outside ☐ inside ☐

**5**

When is it the hottest?
Put the thermometer outside. Every hour go outside and read the thermometer. Write down the temperature.

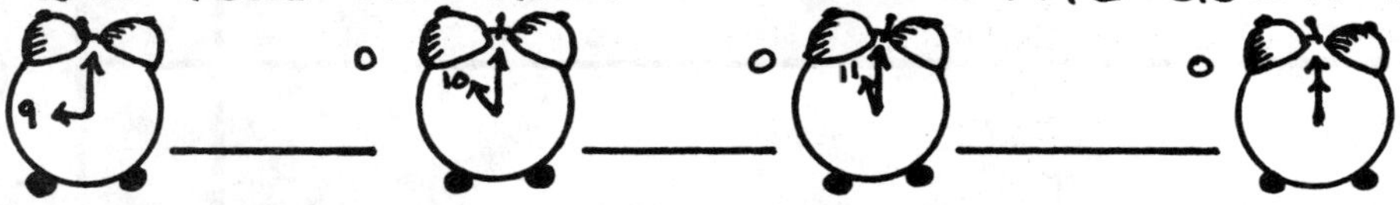

______° ______° ______° ______°

**6**

You need: 

Fill each glass with 1/2 cup of water. Mark where the water came in the glass with a marker. Put one glass in a bright place, the other glass in a dark place. Each day check the glasses. What happens? Why?

# WEATHER CHART

WEATHERMAN ______________________

| MONDAY | TUESDAY | WEDNESDAY | THURSDAY | FRIDAY |
|---|---|---|---|---|
| | | | | |

*Presented to:*

______________________________

*Date:*

______________

**OUTSTANDING WEATHER REPORT AWARD**

______________________________

*Official Signature:*

# LEAVES

## OBJECTIVES

This center is designed to use activities involving sorting, ordering, measuring, writing, and fine motor skills. These actvities focus on the theme, leaves.

## CENTER DISPLAY

Provide an attractive display of fall symbols under a colorful fall bulletin board. Children can help you to gather such things as leaves, acorns, nuts, magazine pictures depicting fall, and vegetables such as Indian corn, pumpkins, squash, and zucchini. Books about the season, as well as stuffed animals (squirrels and owls), can also be attractive additions.

## BULLETIN BOARD

Have the children finger-paint or you paint a large brown tree on butcher paper. This can be cut out and pinned to an orange butcher paper background. As the children complete their sponge-painted leaves, they can be added to the tree. Children may also add pictures of animals (squirrels, etc.) to the bulletin board. Contracts to the Leaf Center may be displayed in a box pinned to the board.

## CONTRACTS

Children may do the center tasks in any order. As a child completes a task and is checked off by the teacher, he may color in the leaf corresponding to the task number.

# MATERIAL

* contract for each child
* magnifying glasses
* Leaf Discovery Worksheet, one per child
* rulers
* sponges cut into inch cubes
* newspaper to cover a large table for painting
* red, yellow, orange poster paint in pie tins
* tagboard leaf templates
* white drawing paper cut 8½" × 11"
* Leaf Stories Shapebook -- at **least** one writing page for each child
* white drawing paper 11" × 18"
* crayons
* pencils
* scissors

## PAINT CENTER

Have a designated paint center in the room. Cover the tables with the newspaper. Provide pie tins half filled with fall colors—orange, yellow, red, and brown paint. Children first make sponge paintings on the 8½" × 11" paper. When the paintings are dry, each child may trace around the tagboard leaf template with pencil and then cut out the leaf shape. These leaves may then be pinned to the brown tree on the bulletin board.

# FALL WALKS

Provide each child with a paper bag. On a special class excursion around the school grounds, children may gather fall leaves to place in the center display.

# LEAVES

BY ______________________

**1** Look carefully at all the leaves in the folder. Sort the leaves into groups that are alike. Can you think of a different way?

**2** Use the magnifying glass. Look carefully at a leaf. Draw and write about what you see.

**3** Use the ruler.
The longest leaf is _ inches long ☐
The shortest leaf is _ inches long. ☐
Take 7 leaves. Place them in order from shortest to longest.

**4** LEAF PAINTING! Use the sponges.
Make a sponge painting on the white paper using fall leaf colors. When you are done, trace around the leaf with a marker. Pin leaf to tree.

**5** Pretend you are a leaf blowing in the wind. Where does the wind take you? Who do you see? Write a story in the leaf book.

**6** LEAF RUBBINGS! Put several leaves under typing paper — vein side up. Rub back and forth across the paper with chalk. Use fall colors.

# LEAF DISCOVERIES

**DISCOVERER:** ______________________

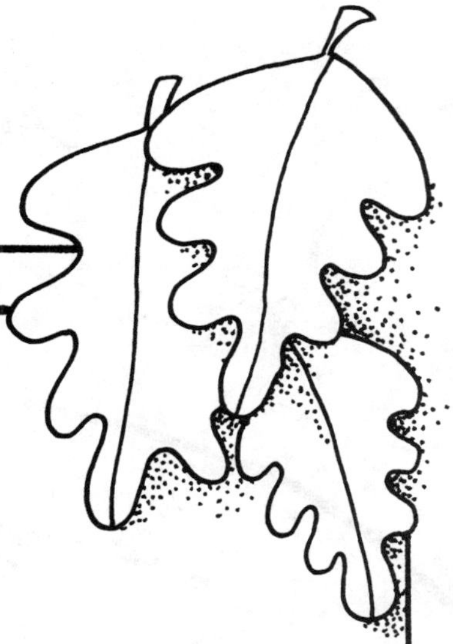

I SAW

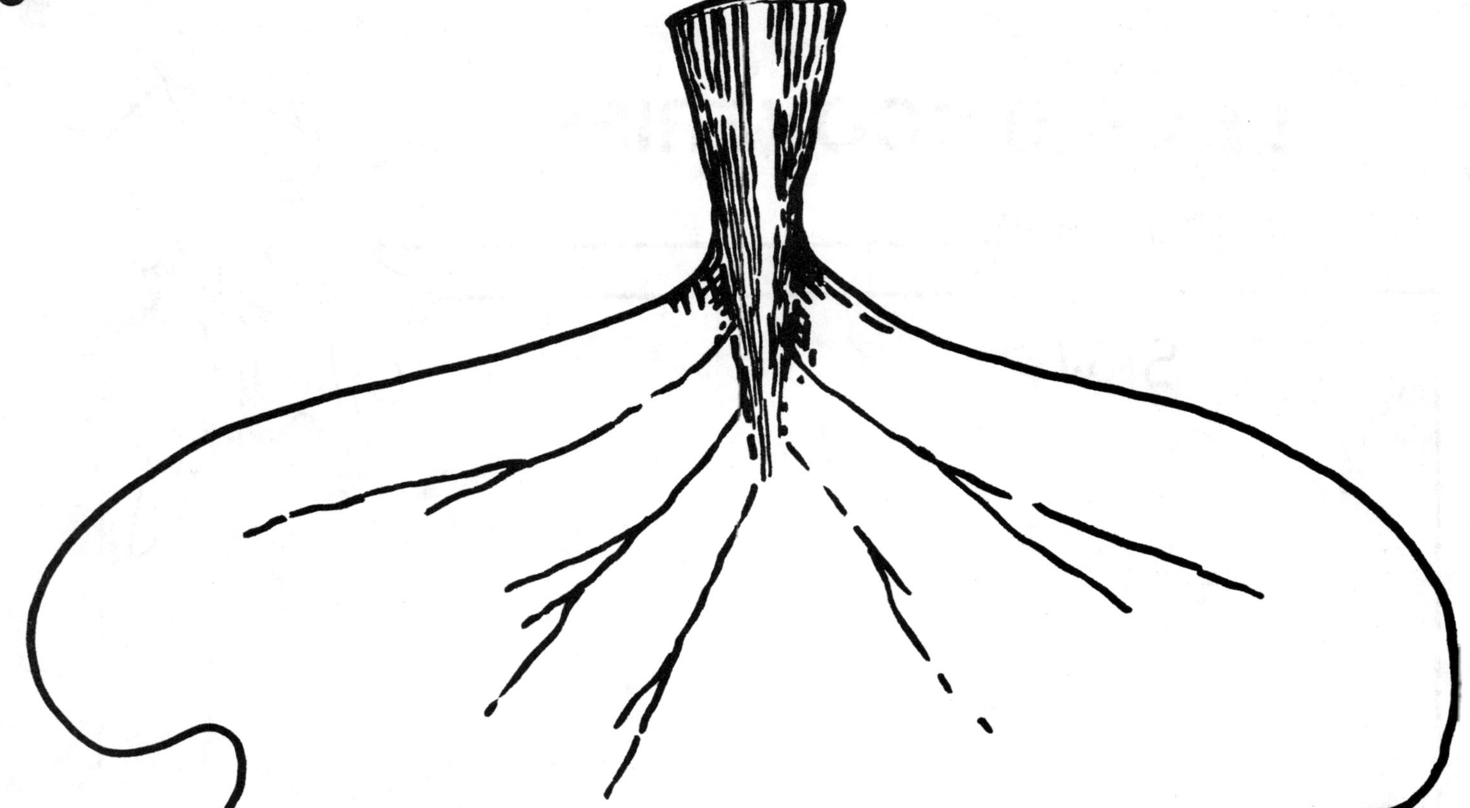

This leaf pattern is to use with activities #4 and #5 on student contract. Additional information below.

LEAF PAINTINGS. Cut leaf pattern (slightly smaller) out of tagboard or light cardboard. Students can use this pattern to trace around dried sponge paintings.

LEAF BOOKS. Trace this leaf pattern onto sheets of yellow, orange and red construction paper. Use for front and back of Leaf Books. Staple with leaf shaped writing paper between covers.

# SCIENCE MINI-CENTER

## PURPOSE

**To help children develop observation skills and foster vocabulary development.**

## MATERIALS

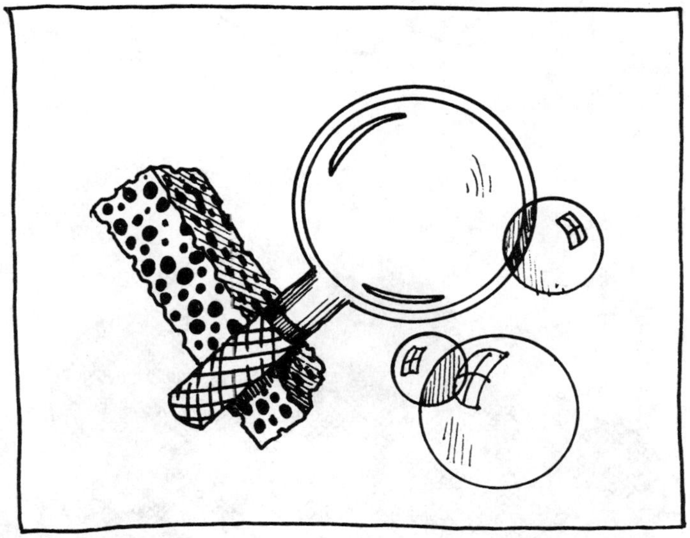

* observation sheets (one for each child)
* magnifying glasses
* microscope (if available)
* weekly object to observe
* class record-keeping list
* pie tin ½ filled with water (float/sink)

## PROCEDURE

Each week, set out a new object at a designated Observation Center for children to observe and record their discoveries. Each week, objects should be different in substance, shape and purpose. The first observations may be done as a class or in small groups to acquaint the children with the Observation Sheet and vocabulary. Each week, the same form should be used. Children place their completed forms in a specified box. They will be recorded by the teacher.

## OBSERVATION OBJECT IDEAS

| | | |
|---|---|---|
| sponges | bubbles | thimbles |
| rocks | blocks | chalk |
| small ball | pencils | plants |
| ruler | wood | eye dropper |
| scissors | glass | plastic container |
| marble | paper | funnel |
| soap | cork | foam rubber |
| clay ball | coins | a friend |

Natural Science

## MATERIALS:

Wind task cards (laminated).
Wind Contract for each child.
Record player, listening post or tape recorder
Pencils, crayons, scissors, stapler
Bulletin board display _ background of blue butcher paper, white cotton clouds, black lettering.
Children will add construction paper kites.

## PURPOSE:

To acquaint students with the properties of wind through observation and experimentation.

# PROCEDURE

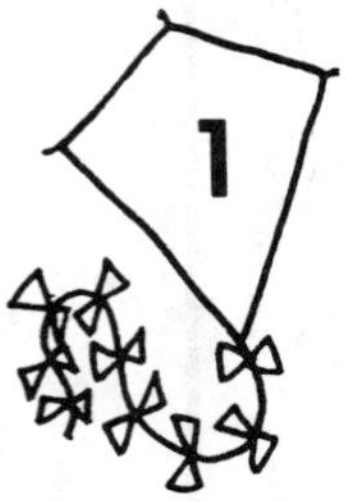


*Provide three kite patterns made from tagboard for the children to trace.

*Variety of colored construction paper, pre-cut 11" × 9." Lightweight writing paper also will be needed. Children will write their own "Wind Journal." Following each task, the children will write their observations in their books. At the top of each page, have them write the number of the previously made task card they completed. A display is helpful.

*Provide the book Gilberto and the Wind by Marie Ets, Viking Press. The record is also available if you have children unable to read the book, you also can tape the story on a cassette.

*Children will again use the tagboard kite patterns and the 11" × 9" construction paper. Also provide crepe paper and yarn. Scraps of construction paper can be used to decorate the kites. Each child pins his/her kite to the bulletin board.

*Children will write in the kite books from task one.

*Children will use Gilberto and the Wind to observe how artists portray windy days (wavy lines). Perhaps they can also discover this in other classroom books.

*A pinwheel worksheet is needed for each child. A display made by the teacher also will be helpful. Children can provide pencils with erasers from home. Plastic straws will also work. Long straight pins are needed.

*Provide corks, thumbtacks, toothpicks and light paper. A small bowl or tub half filled with water should be placed on foam, or in a low pan to catch any water leakage. Sailboat races can be a special part of the center with the winner receiving a special award.

* A long piece of cloth can be tied to a long stick and stuck in the ground outside the classroom. Children should observe the stick at least three different times of the day.

# EXTRAS

* Children can portray windy days in movement experiences with their bodies such as:

—a leaf falling from a tree.
—a cloud moving gently in the sky.
—smoke coming out of chimneys.
—dirt in a dust storm.
—people.
—a kite in the sky.
—clothes hanging on a line.
—sailboats.
—trees and flowers.

It is fun to move to the tempo of a record. With body movements becoming brisk with the increase in wind (faster music), and subsiding with the wind and gently moving with the decrease (slower music).

* Children also can portray movement through finger painting and free drawing.
* Blowing on balloons (already inflated and tied) to watch movement pattern, also can be interesting.

# WIND

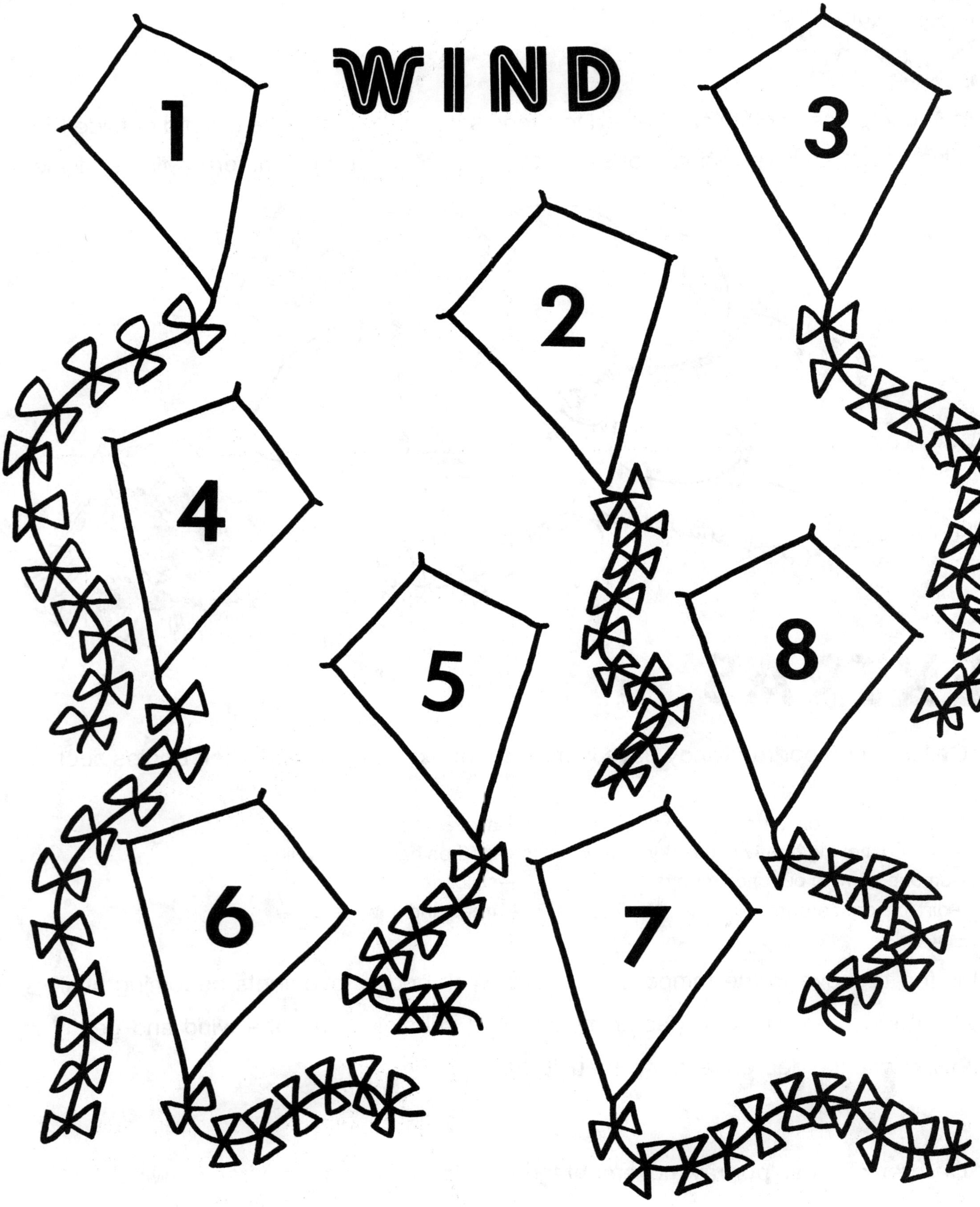


Name ______________________________

* NOTE TO TEACHER

Kite pattern will be used in all activities in wind section.

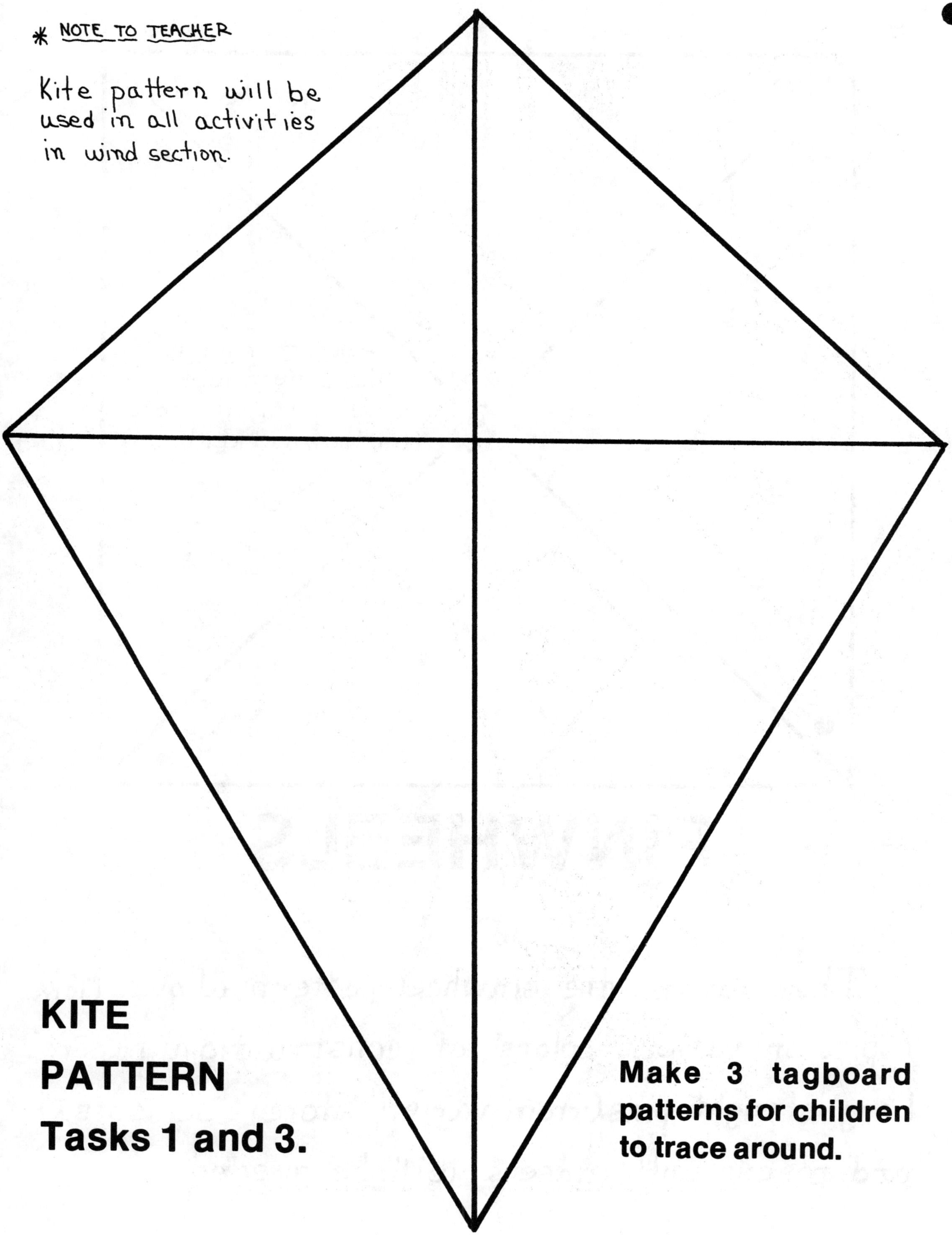

**KITE PATTERN**

**Tasks 1 and 3.**

**Make 3 tagboard patterns for children to trace around.**

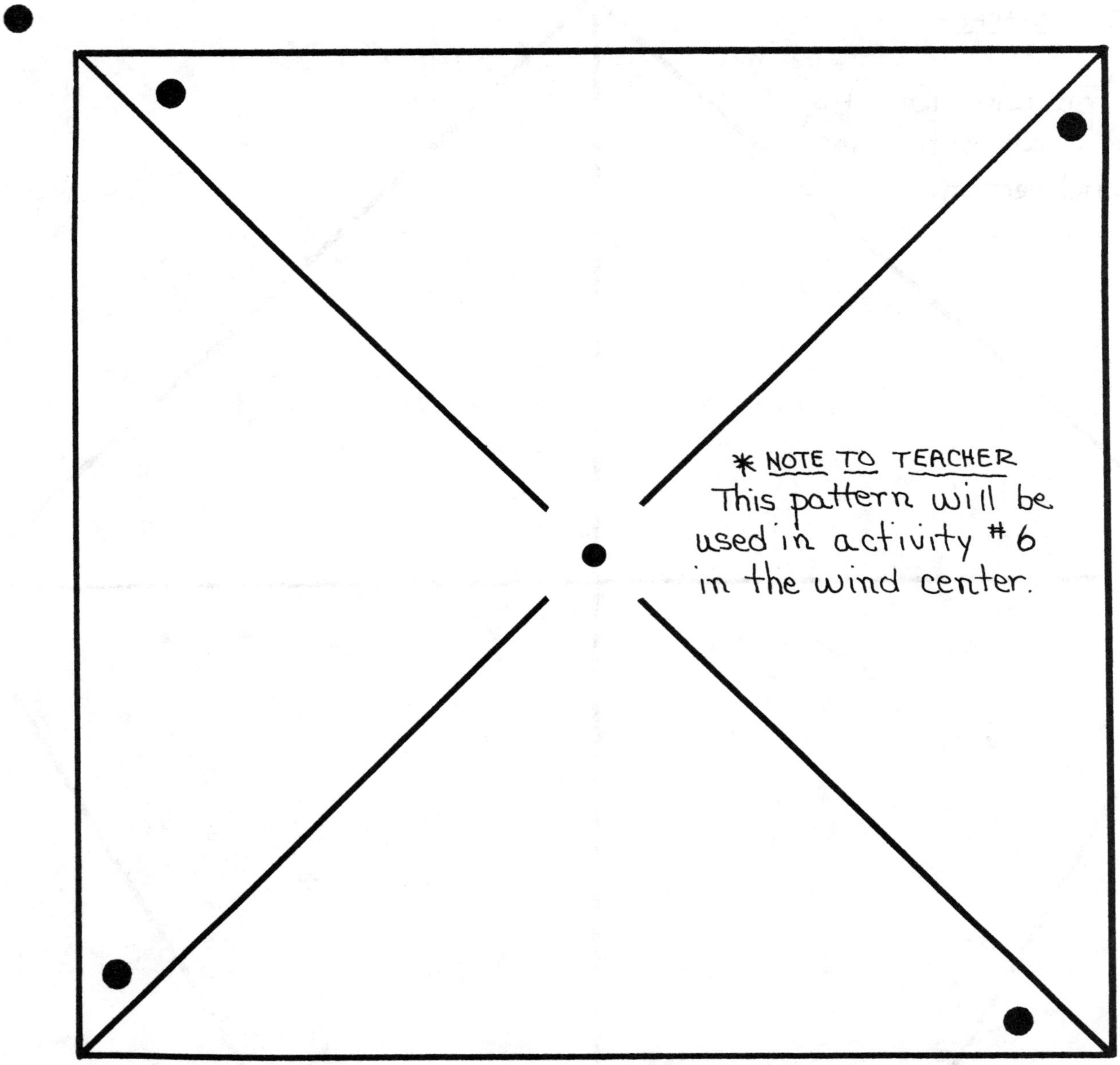


# PINWHEELS

Thermofax the pinwheel pattern above. Make copies on various colors of construction paper. Long straight pins (from variety store), scissors, and pencils with erasers will be needed.

# KITE BOOKS

1 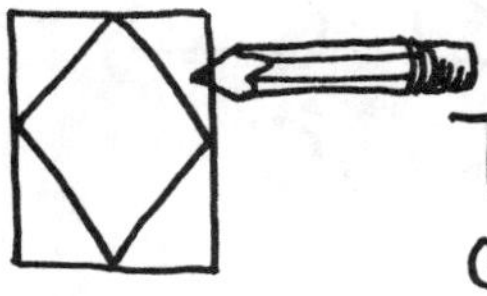
Trace the kite pattern on construction paper. Do this two times.

2 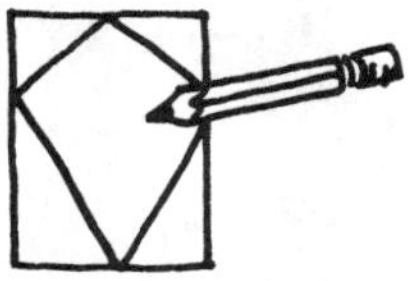
Draw the outline of the kite pattern on 6 pieces of writing paper.

3 
Cut out all the kite shapes that you have traced.

4 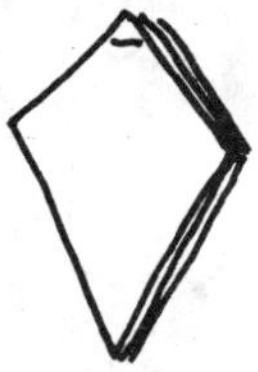
Place the writing pages inbetween the 2 cover pages and staple at the top.

5 
Decorate the cover of your book. Put your name on the cover. After trying every task, you will write in this book.

## GILBERTO AND THE WIND

1 Listen carefully to the story <u>Gilberto and the Wind</u>.

* <u>NOTE TO TEACHER</u> Make a tape recording of the story. Students may read along as they listen.

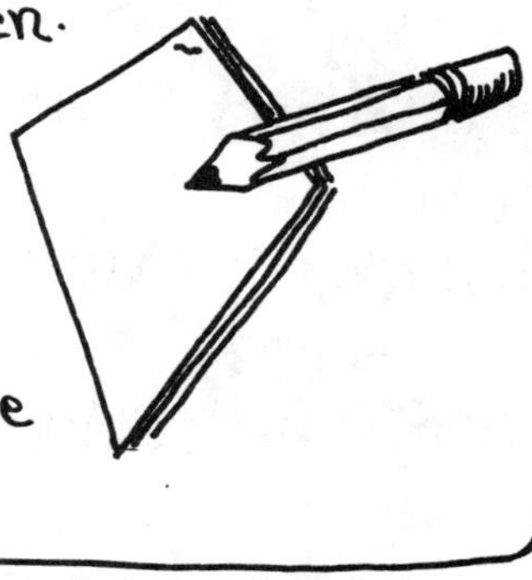

2 In your kite book, write what you liked about the story. Why did the author title the story <u>Gilberto and the Wind</u>?

## HOW TO MAKE A KITE

3

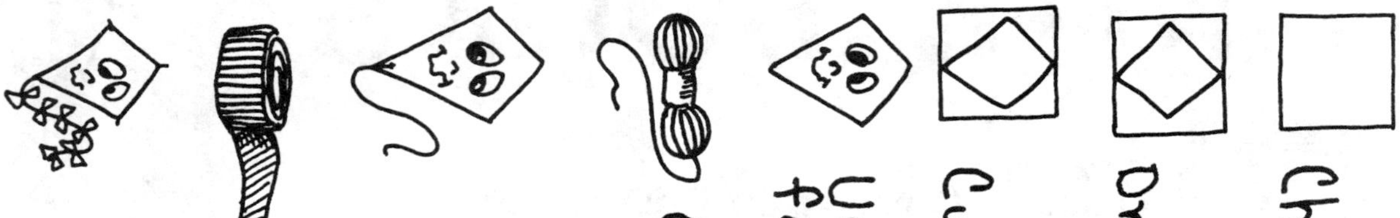

1. Choose a kite pattern.
2. Draw around pattern.
3. Cut it out.
4. Use crayons to draw a face on the kite.
5. Cut a piece of yarn as long as your arm.
6. Staple the yarn to the bottom of the kite face.
7. Cut pieces of crepe paper.
8. Twist the crepe paper around the yarn to make bows.

## KITE STORY

4

Pretend you are a kite flying high in the sky. The wind is pushing you gently along. What do you see and where do you go? Write in your kite book.

# WINDY PICTURES

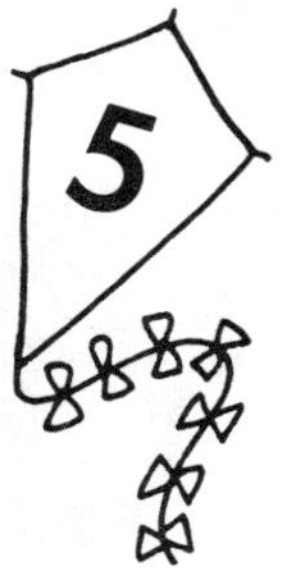


1 Look carefully at the pictures in the book Gilberto and the Wind.

2 How did the person who drew the pictures (the illustrator) show that it was a windy day?

3 Draw a windy picture in your kite book.

4 Write about the picture you drew.

# PINWHEELS

1 Take a copy of the pinwheel worksheet. Cut carefully on the lines almost to the center.

2 Without creasing the paper, pin each point to the center. Only the points with • dots

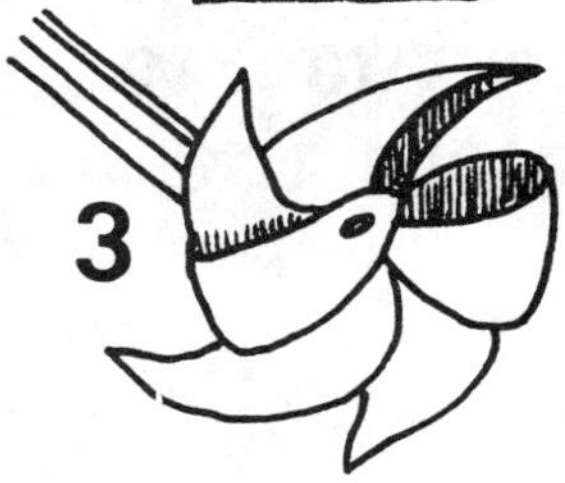

3 Push the  pin into the eraser end of a pencil. 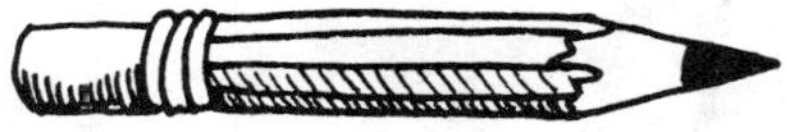

4 What makes the pinwheel turn? Blow on it. Run with it. Write what you learn in kite book.

# SAILBOATS

1 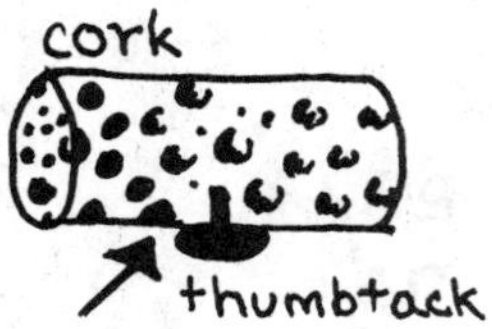


Push a thumbtack into the middle of a cork.

2 

Cut a triangular shaped sail from paper. Thread a toothpick through the sail as shown.

3 

Carefully stick sail into the cork.

4 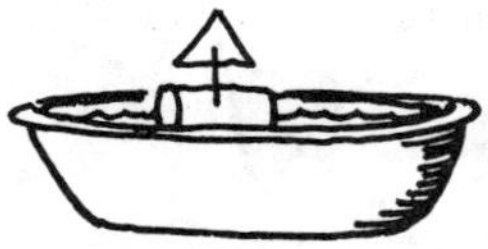

Place cork boat in water. Does it move? How? What happens when you blow? Write what you learn in your kite book.

# OBSERVING WIND

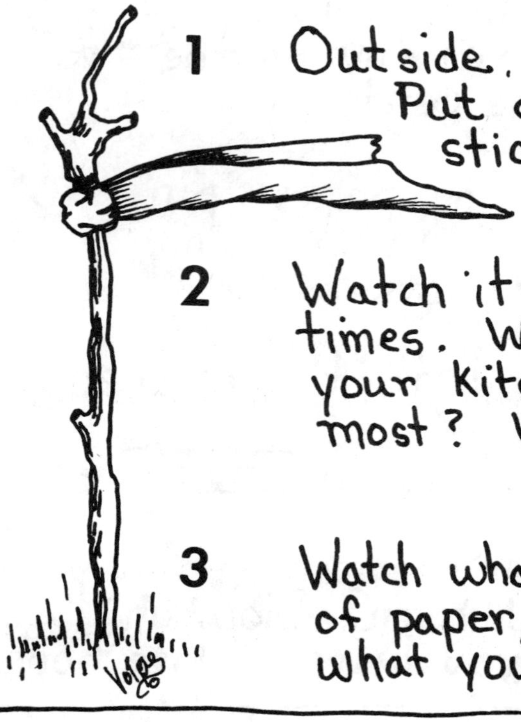

1 Outside, put a stick in the ground. Put a long strip of cloth on the stick.

2 Watch it carefully, at least 3 different times. Write what you see each time in your kite book. When did it blow the most? Why?

3 Watch what the wind does to: trees, pieces of paper, dust, clothing. Write about what you see in your kite book.

# PLANTS

## PURPOSE

To understand two of the basic needs of plants — water and light.

To understand that there are three parts to each seed — the seed coat, a baby plant, and some stored food.

## DISPLAY

Assemble an attractive center display on a table near a bulletin board. On a large piece of white butcher paper, have children finger paint a green grass background scene. This paper may be tacked to the bulletin board. As children complete their crepe paper flowers, they may be added to the background.

## MATERIALS

Plant contract for each child.
Packages of lima beans.
Magnifying glasses.
Bean plant worksheet for each child.
Lid from jars to soak beans in.

Children should use the magnifying glass to find where the roots, stem and leaves grow on the plant. Have children try the same experiment with other kinds of seeds. Do the baby plants always look the same?

2 paper cups for each child (sections from egg cartons or milk cartons saved from their lunch also will work.)

lima bean or radish seeds

teaspoon

eye dropper

Soil stored in a coffee can or ice cream barrel.

Children should write their observations on the Plant Observation Worksheet.

Calendar Worksheet for each child. Children should fill in the appropriate planting dates in the calendar squares. They can make notations for such things as watering, measuring and any growth. Additional observations can be written on the Plant Observation Worksheet.

2 paper cups, milk cartons or egg carton sections for each child.

soil

teaspoon markers for watering.

lima bean or radish seeds

Children should make their observations on the Plant Observation Worksheet.

Observations also can be noted on the Calendar Worksheet.

Make 3 or 4 flower patterns out of tagboard for children to trace. Patterns should be 9" × 9".

Children trace around the pattern on colored construction paper, cut it out, and write their names on the back.

Use 2" × 2" squares of brightly colored crepe paper. These can be stored in coffee cans or shoe boxes at the center. Children lightly wrap the crepe paper, piece by piece, around their pencil erasers. Put the eraser in the center of the crepe paper square. Lightly bring up all the sides wrapping the eraser. Put a dab of paste on the bottom of the paper. Attach it to the flower pattern. Continue until the flower is completely covered. Pin the flowers on the bulletin board.

Precut 9" × 13" strips of brightly colored construction paper. Display these at the center.

Children can collect flowers and leaves from around the school and home. Put the nature collectables vein-side up under the strip of paper. With crayons, color back and forth on top, until the leaves and flowers appear as an imprint. Punch a hole in the top of the strip of paper. Tie a yarn bow in the top of the strip. Put the new bookmark in your favorite book.

# PLANTS

NAME DATE

**1**

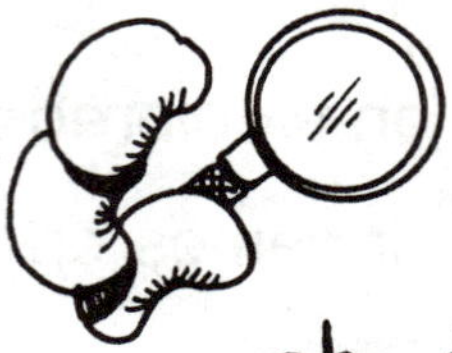

Overnight, soak 3 lima beans in water.

Use bean plant worksheet. Discover what the inside of a bean looks like.

**2**

You need 

WHAT HAPPENS?

Fill 2 cups with dirt. Mark one cup "A", the other "B". Place 3 seeds 1/4" under dirt in each cup. Each day put 1 teaspoon water in cup "A" and 2 drops water in cup "B".

**3**

Keep a calendar graph on cup 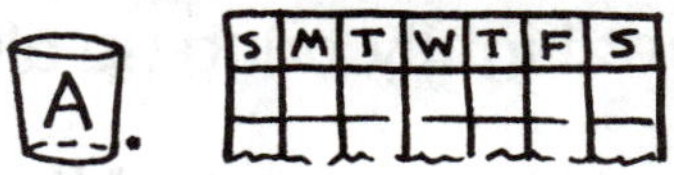


Draw a picture of what you see each day.

Measure your plant each day. Record the measurement.

**4**

You need: 

WHAT HAPPENS?

Fill 2 cups with dirt. Mark one cup "C" the other cup "D." In each cup put 3 seeds 1/4" under the soil. Put 1 teaspoon of water in each cup each day. Put cup "C" by window, cup "D" in closet.

**5**

On construction paper trace around the flower pattern. Cut it out. Wad squares of crepe paper into ball shapes. Paste on the flower pattern. Cover it completely.

**6**

You need 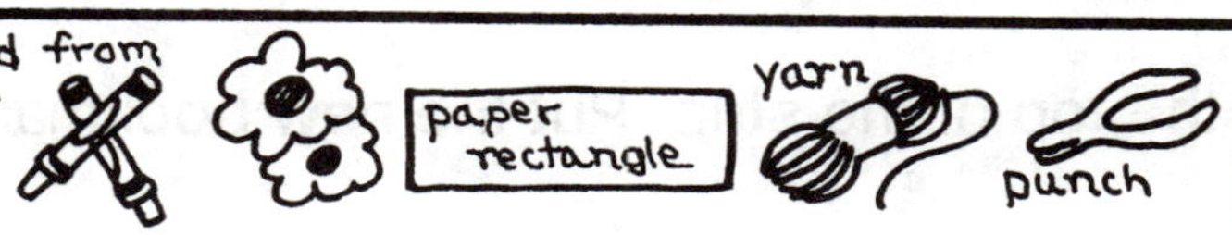

Lay your collectables, vein-side up under a piece of thin paper. Rub crayons back and forth. Punch hole in top and tie with yarn bow.

# OBSERVING BEAN PLANTS

**OBSERVER** ______________________________

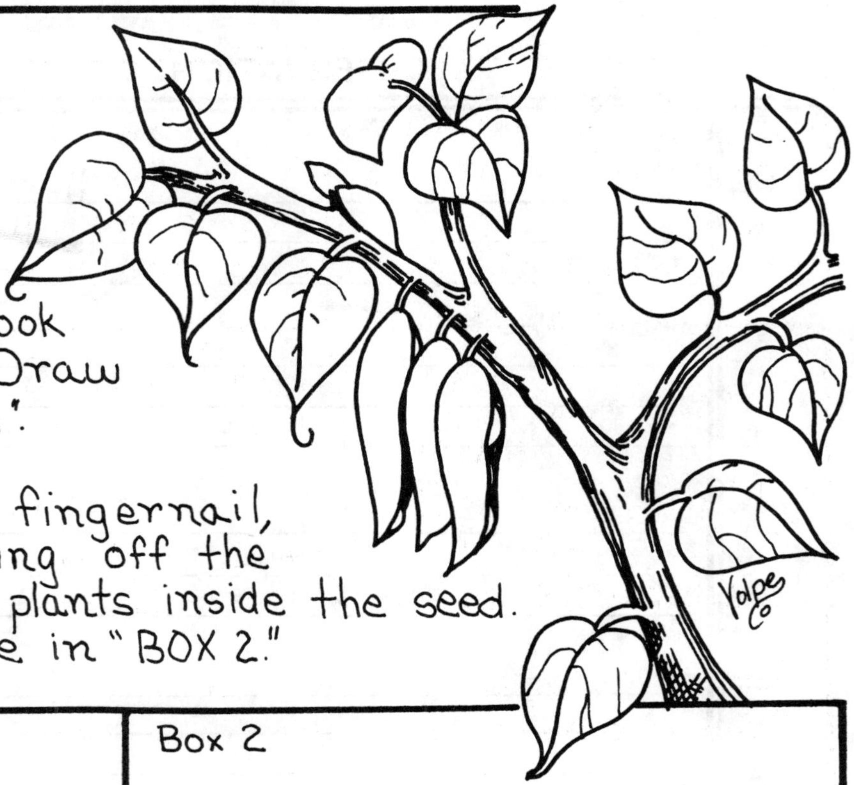

Where do beans come from?

Be a super detective. Use the magnifying glass and look carefully at the bean. Draw what you see in "BOX 1".

Carefully, with your fingernail, take the outer covering off the bean. Study the baby plants inside the seed. Draw what you see in "BOX 2."

| Box 1 | Box 2 |
|---|---|
| | |

Tell about your discoveries.

______________________________

______________________________

# PLANT OBSERVATION

OBSERVER ______________________

DATE OBSERVATION

# PLANT CHART

**Draw what your plant looks like each day. Measure your plant.**

| SUNDAY | MONDAY | TUESDAY | WEDNESDAY | THURSDAY | FRIDAY | SATURDAY |
|---|---|---|---|---|---|---|
| | | | | | | |
| | | | | | | |
| | | | | | | |
| | | | | | | |

# Feeling Box

## Purpose :

To develop tactile perceptual skills.

## Material :

* grocery store box converted into the portable "Feeling Box".
* Feeling Box contract for each child
* blindfolds
* Mystery Box
* activity envelopes numbered for each task.
* coffee cans labeled on the outside with objects inside to feel.

# Mystery Box

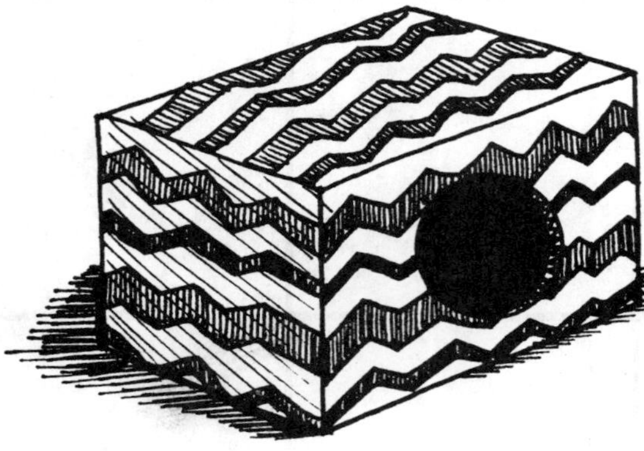

Colorfully decorate a grocery store box with colored contact paper or paint. Cut a hole in one side of the box large enough for a child to insert his hand. The original box top can be left on and slit on three sides for easy accessibility.

# Collage in Nature

LOOK carefully at nature materials (seeds, leaves, sticks, flowers, etc.). Feel each one. Arrange them on heavy paper with glue. How do they feel?

## 2 PAIRS

You need: 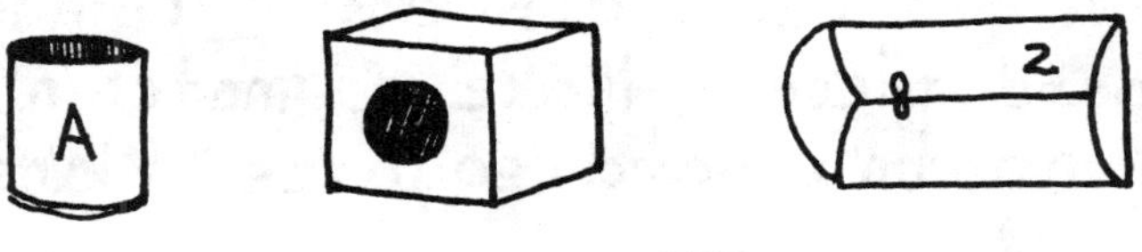


A. Put the materials in can 

in the 

B. Put the materials in the 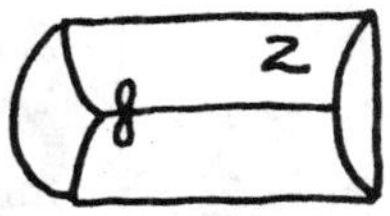

on the table.

C. Put your  inside the 
Feel carefully. Can you feel the material on the 

Can you find each pair?

NOTE TO TEACHER:

Cut large squares of matching textured material such as burlap, velvet, lace, satin, denim, and fur. Place one piece of each pair in the activity envelope and the other in can "A".

## 3 HOW MANY?

You need: 

bean cards number cards

A. Put the 

bean cards in the .

B. Put the 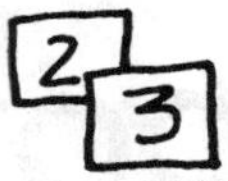

number cards on the table.

C. Put your  inside the 
Feel the material on the table carefully. Count the number of beans BBB on the 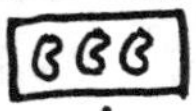

. Find the number card on the table that shows how many beans are on your card.

BBB 3 Were you right?

NOTE TO TEACHER:

Glue different combinations of beans on cardboard pieces. Make a matching number of number cards on tagboard squares. Place all of them in envelope ③.

## 4 HARD OR SOFT?

You need: 

A. Put the materials in 

in the 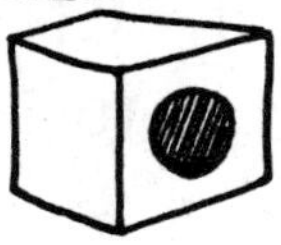

B.  Feel each thing carefully. If it is soft put it on the 

C. If it is hard put it on the 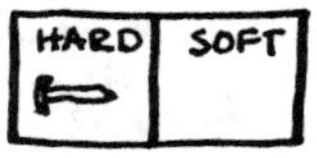


NOTE TO TEACHER:

Assemble objects that feel either hard or soft in can "D". Soft objects could include: cotton, fur, silk, feathers, yarn balls, stuffed animals, a sock. Hard things could include: nail, pencil, nut, rock, ruler, scissors, Make a hard/soft chart out of tagboard. This can be folded in half and numbered "4" on the outside to be included in the portable center box.

## 5 ROUGH OR SMOOTH?

You need: 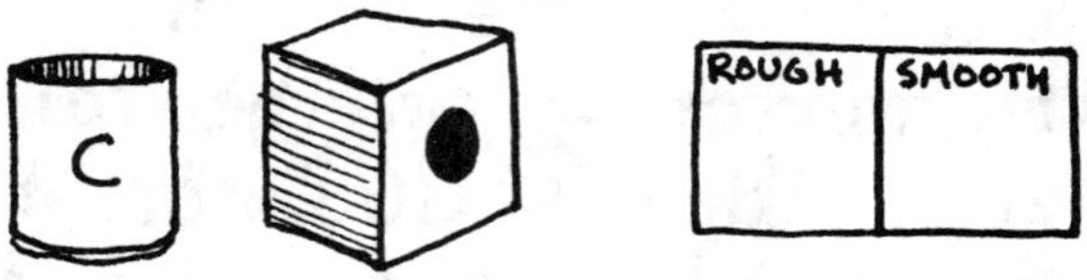


A. Put the materials in 

in the 

B.  Feel each thing carefully. If it is rough, put it on the 

C. If it is smooth, put it on the 

NOTE TO TEACHER:

Assemble objects that feel rough or smooth in can "C". Rough objects can include sand paper, cross cut board, burlap, basket, brush, screen wire and a file. Smooth items could include glass, metal, fork/spoon, lid, ribbon and plastic wrap. Make a rough/smooth chart from tagboard. This can be folded in half and numbered "5" on the outside and placed in the box.

## 6 ORDERING TEXTURE

You need: 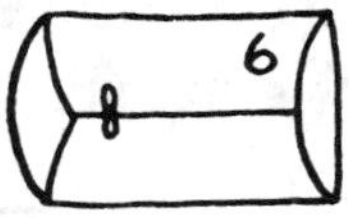

A. Put the materials from 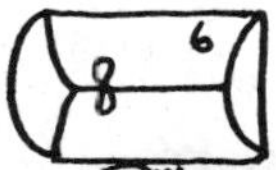

in front of you.

B. Put on the blindfold. 

C. Feel each item carefully. Line the materials from left to right from what you think is the smoothest to what you think is the roughest. Check and see if you are right.

NOTE TO TEACHER:

Assemble objects in the activity envelope that are varying degrees of texture. Such material can include sandpaper, burlap, glass, paper, leather, denim, satin and wood.

## 7 WHAT IS IT MADE OF?

You need: 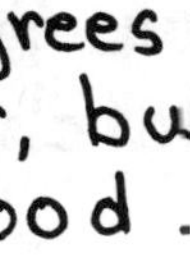

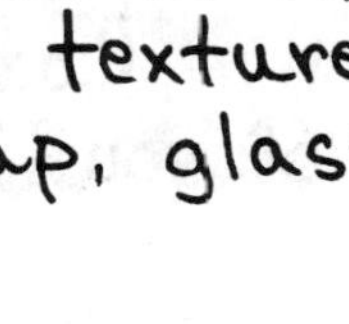
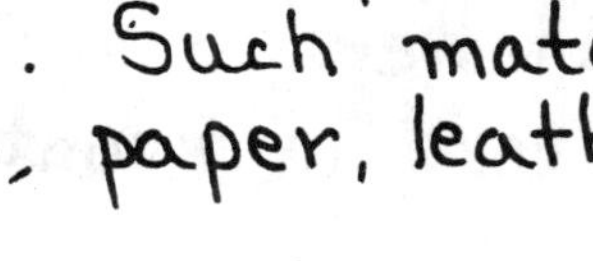


material cards

A. Put the materials in  in 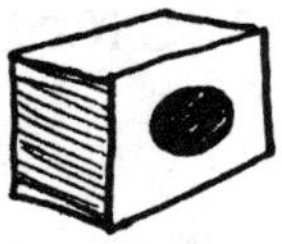

B. Put the 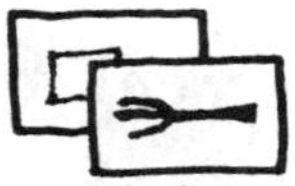 material cards in front of you.

C. Put your  inside the  Feel the material on the card and in the box carefully. Can you find the objects in the  that are made from the same material on the cards? Match them.

NOTE TO TEACHER: Make material cards by gluing objects representing different categories on cardboard. These can include rubber band, plastic fork, glass slide, popsicle stick, paper clip. Find household objects representing each category. Put them in can "B".

## 8 LETTERS

You need: 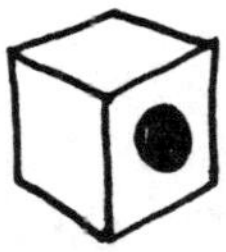 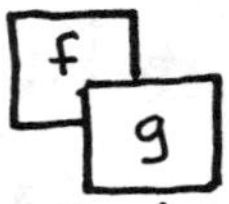 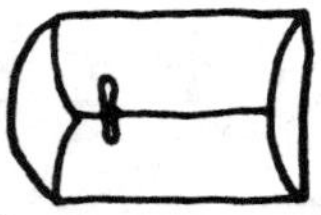 feely letters  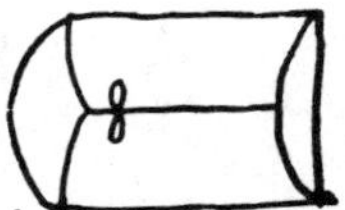 letter cards

A. Put all the  feely letters in the 

B. Put the   letter cards in front of you.

C. Put your  inside the  Feel the letters carefully. Can you find the matching letter card in front of you? Match all the pairs.

NOTE TO TEACHER: Make "feely letters" on cardboard squares. Form the letter shape with white glue. When it dries it will make a raised formation to the touch. Place these "feely letters" in the activity envelope. Make matching letter cards from glue. Place these in another envelope.

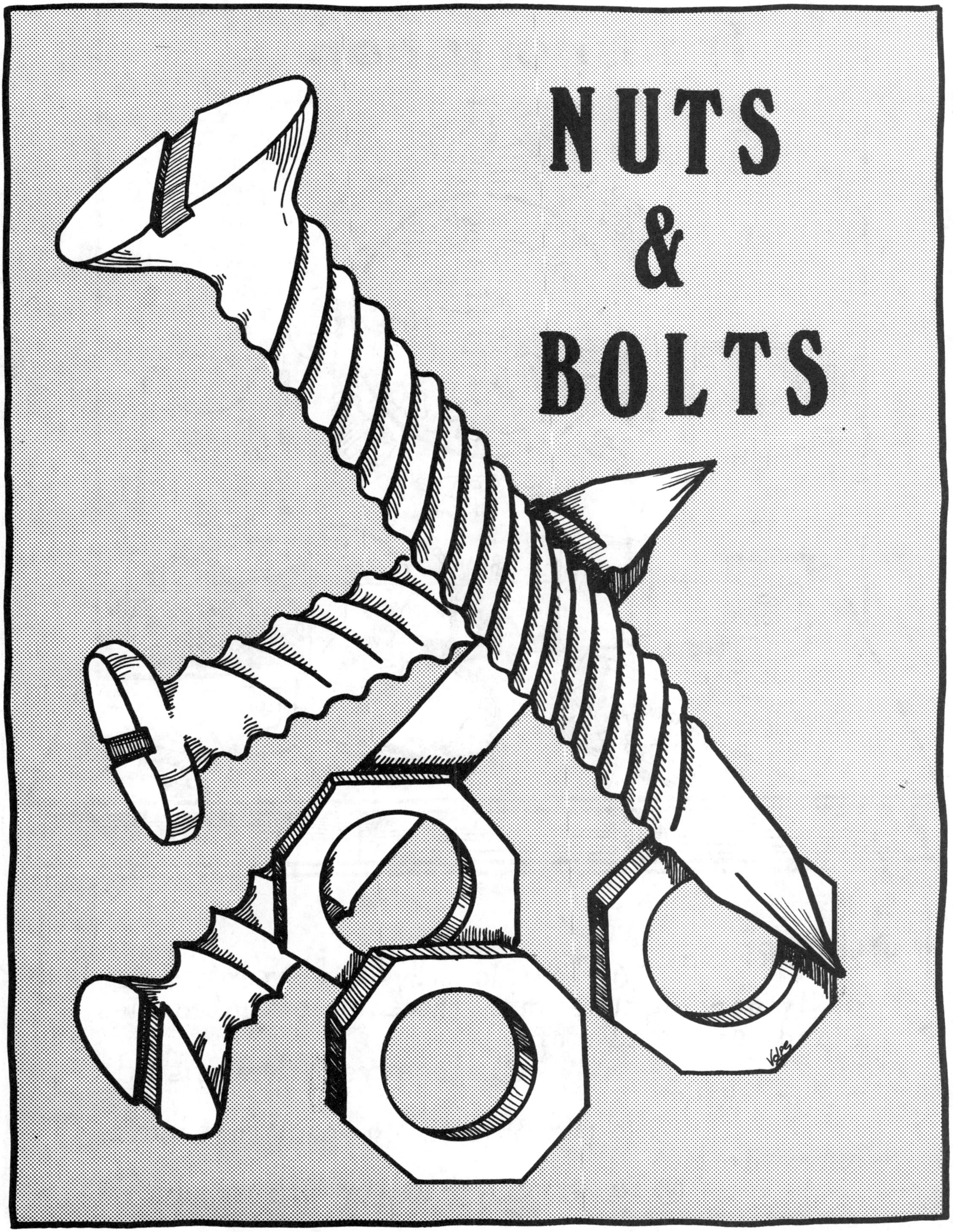
NUTS
&
BOLTS

# Transportation

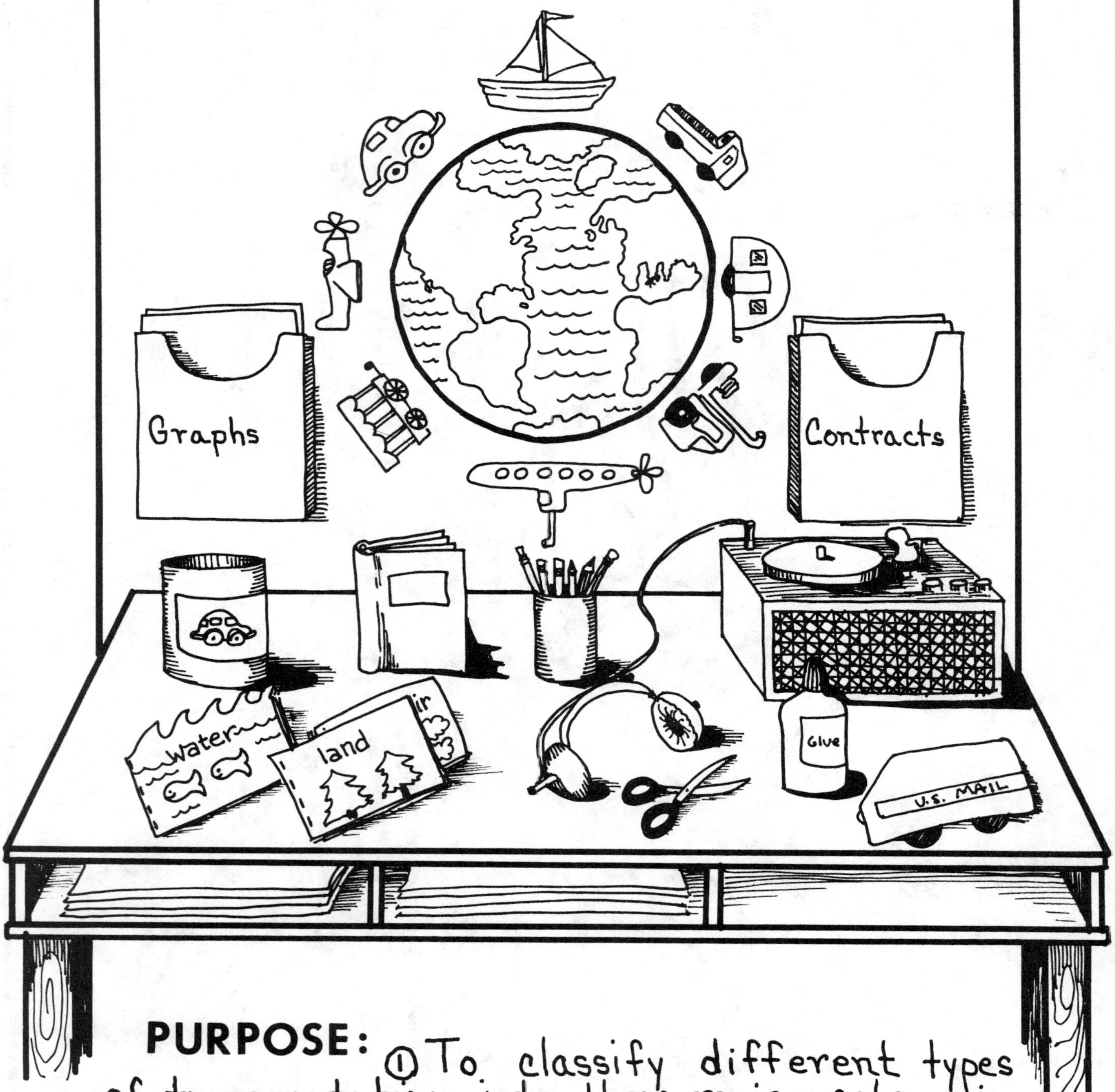


**PURPOSE:** ① To classify different types of transportation into three major categories (land, air, and water).
② To strengthen visual motor skills.
③ To plot objects on and interpret a bar graph.
④ To strengthen writing skills.

# DISPLAY

On a large piece of white butcher paper, have children finger-paint a large world. Green paint can indicate land and blue paint can indicate water. Tack this painting to a brightly colored background. As children complete their milk carton vehicles, they can be pinned around the world.

# MATERIALS

**1**
* Transportation contract for each child.
* Provide 3 truck patterns from tagboard for the children to trace.
* White construction paper to trace the pattern on.
* Scissors, paste, crayons, stapler.
* Blue and red construction paper to use as stripes on the cover.
* Sample of completed U.S. Mail Truck.
* Writing paper - at least 5 sheets per child.
* Children make shape books with U.S. Mail Pattern as the cover.
* Writing paper is cut the same size and stapled inside. Children use the book to write down their stories.

**2**
* Clay sticks for each child.

**3**
* Record player
* Any record-book read-along set pertaining to transportation.

**4**
* Various sizes of milk cartons (washed).
* Scrap paper
* Brads to fasten paper wheels onto carton.
* Scissors, paste

* Cartons may be painted with poster paint. If you add detergent to the paint, it will make the paint adhere to the wax of the carton.
* Teachers will need to help children cut the tops off the cartons.
* Children can make different kinds of transportation objects through experimentation. Seats, steering wheels, license plates, etc., can be added by using construction paper, toothpicks, and spools.

**5**
* Coffee can filled with various small transportation toys available at the variety store.

* Graph worksheet for each child.

**6**
* Old magazines to cut up.
* Paste
* Scissors
* Shape books of water, land, air with plain paper stapled inside.

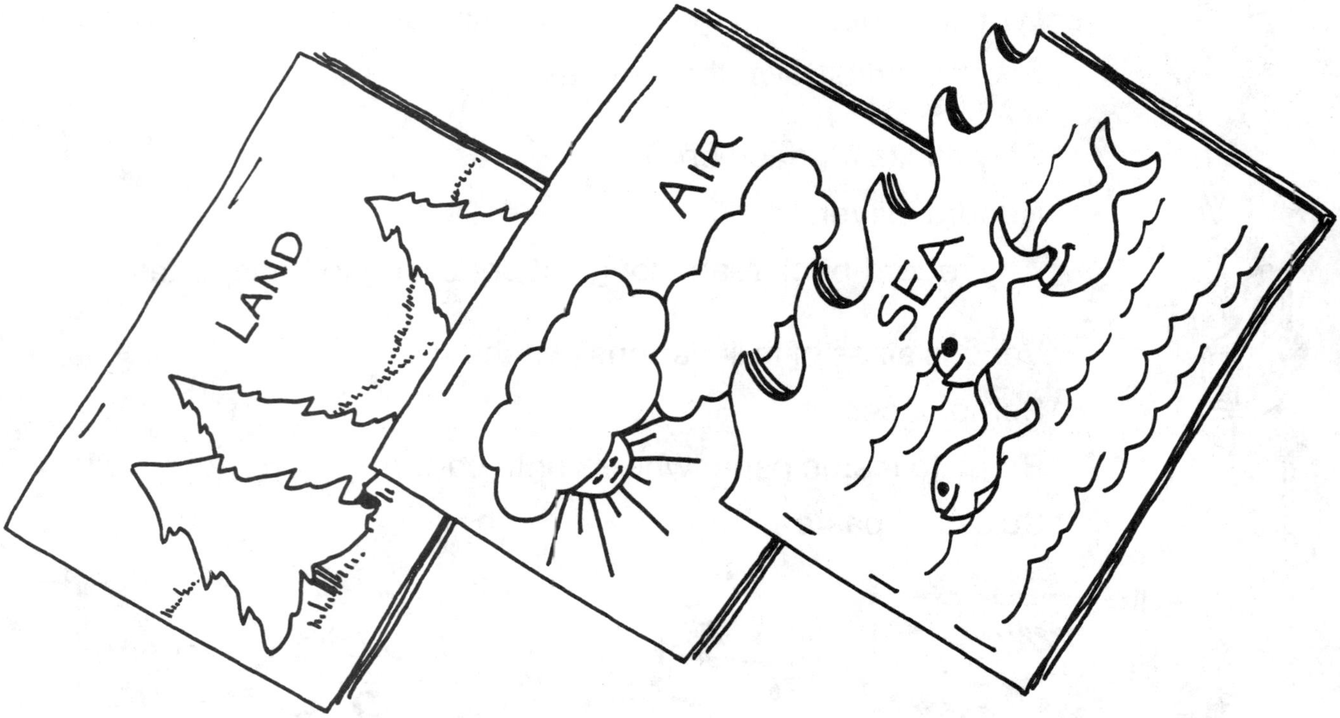

# Transportation

You need: 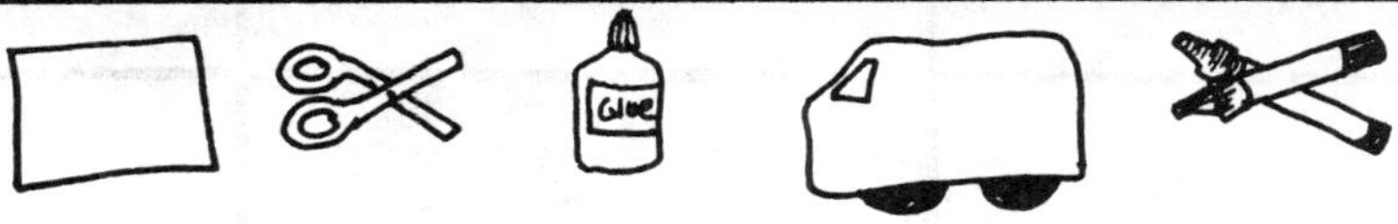


Make a cover for your writing book. Trace the template on the paper. Make a truck just like the sample.

You need:  (clay). Make something out of clay that people ride. Write a story in your book   about what you made.

Listen carefully to the 

 Read along with the book.

Write about what  you heard.

You need: 

Make a milk carton vehicle. Paint it. Write a story about it in your book.

You need a  (car can) 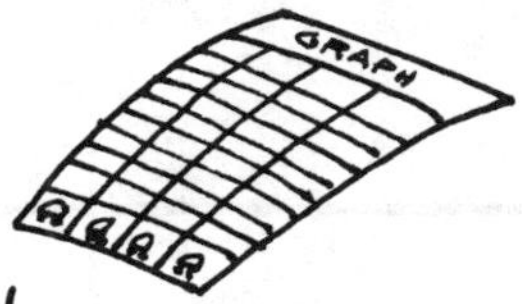


Graph the kinds of things that people ride. Write about your discoveries  in your book.

Look through magazines. Cut out transportation pictures. Paste the pictures in the correct scrapbook. Name them.

# Transportation Graphing

| | | | | |
|---|---|---|---|---|
| 12 | | | | |
| 11 | | | | |
| 10 | | | | |
| 9 | | | | |
| 8 | | | | |
| 7 | | | | |
| 6 | | | | |
| 5 | | | | |
| 4 | | | | |
| 3 | | | | |
| 2 | | | | |
| 1 | | | | |
| |  trucks | 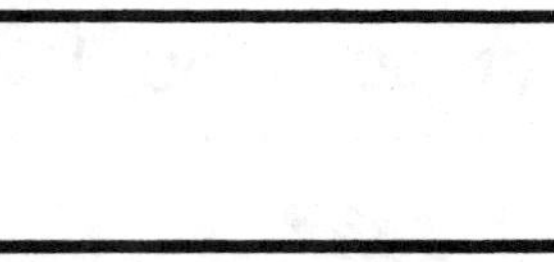 planes | 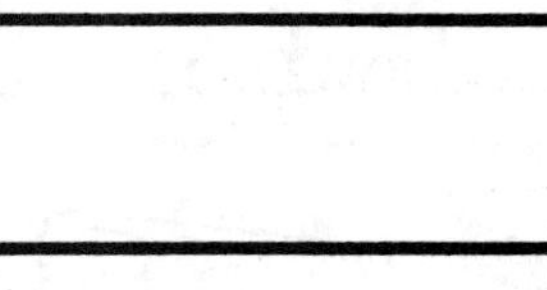 cars | 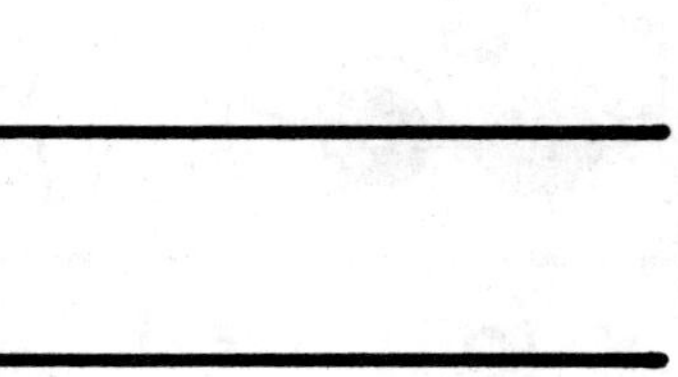 boats |

Add 2 black construction paper wheels.

*NOTE TO TEACHER: Pattern could be placed on master and duplicated. Students cut and paste and color details.

# MACHINES

## PURPOSE:

To familiarize children with the usefulness of machines and energy.

To help develop observation and writing techniques on the theme, "machines."

## MATERIALS:

* One machine contract for each child.
* Display table for the study about machines.
* Pictures of machines.
* Library books about machines and energy.
* Machines for children to experiment with.
* Legos and Tinker Toys as optional projects to build machines with and to keep on the display table.
* Sign-up sheet for children who would like to pantomime to the class an imaginary or real machine (may do this as a group or as an individual).
* One "Machine Book" for each child. This can be made by the children, or an aide, by folding an 18" X 11" piece of construction paper in half. Inside, writing paper can be stapled to make the pages in the book. Children should title their books, "The Machine Book," and put their names on the cover. Childen should write their answers and observations to each task in these books. On the top right hand corner of each page, the task number can be written for easy reference.

Children may do the tasks in any order.

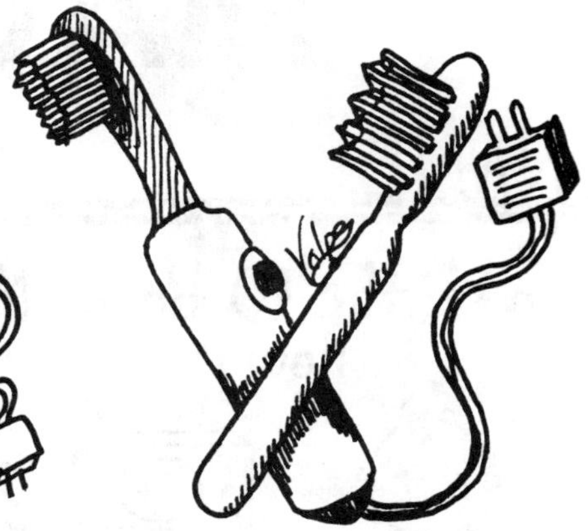

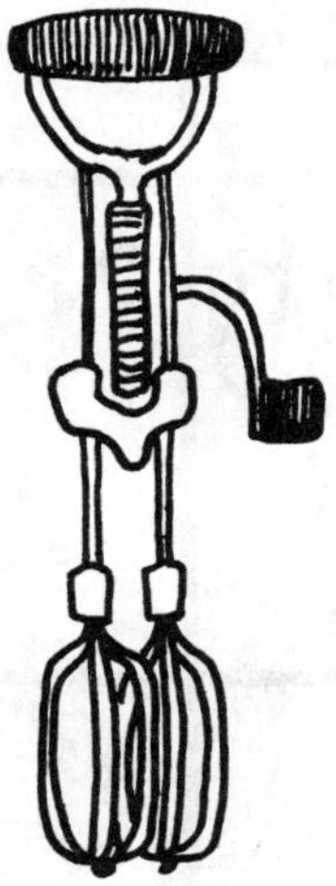

## PROCEDURE:

**1** In a large box, place matching portable and electric objects:
portable radio/electric radio
ordinary toothbrush/electric toothbrush
paper fan/electric fan
portable typewriter/electric typewriter
flashlight/electric lamp
eggbeater/electric handmixer
teakettle/electric coffee pot
wind-up clock/electric clock

Children should have ample time to experience the objects.

**2** box of magazines
scissors
paste

**3** Machine Book and pencil
A class list of machine names can also be displayed at the center.

**4** A large box of scraps should be available. The following can be included:
hammer, nails, saw, wood scraps
egg cartons, cardboard, paper towel tubes
material, wallpaper, construction paper scraps
paint, paintbrushes
scissors, paste, crayons, stapler, hole punch
yarn, glitter, sequins

Creativity should be stressed. A special display table for the finished products may be provided. Special awards for "Outstanding Machines" can be given.

**5** Machine Books
pencils

# MACHINES

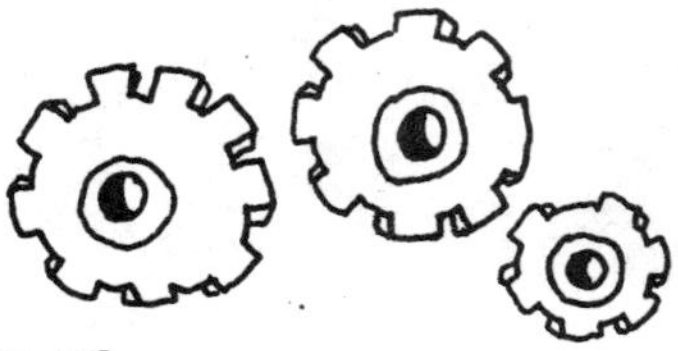

NAME DATE

Take the ① box. Match the objects that go together. 1
How is each set alike? How is each set different?

Write your answers in your MACHINE BOOK.

You need: 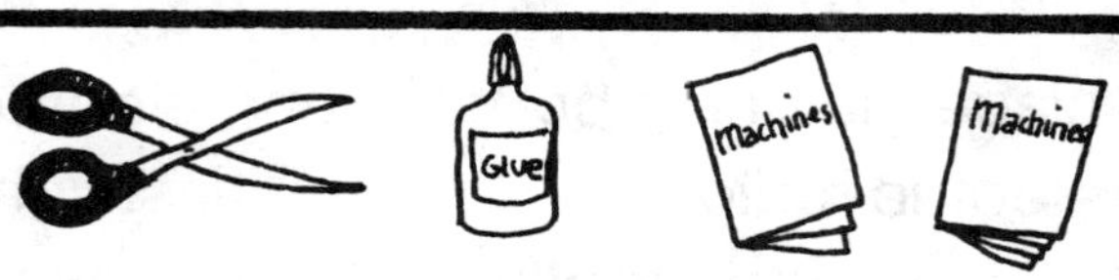

electricity 2

Look through magazines. Cutout pictures of machines that need electricity. Paste the pictures in MACHINE BOOK.

LOOK around the classroom. How many machines can you find that need energy to work? Write the names in your MACHINE BOOK. 3

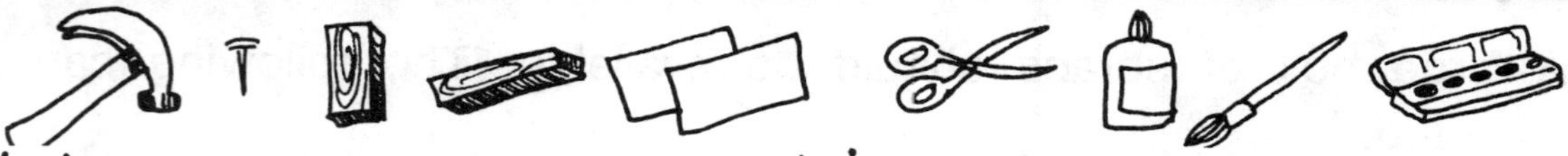 4

Make an imaginary machine. Use scraps, paper or wood. Write a story in your MACHINE BOOK about the machine you make. What is it? How does it work?

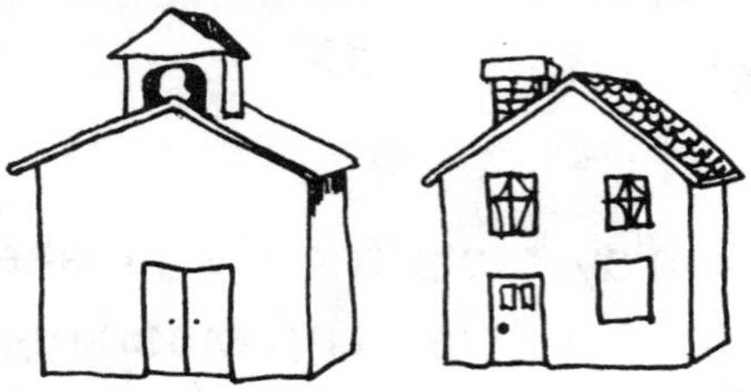

All week look for people using machines in school and at home. Write in your book who the people are and what machine they used. How did it make their work easier? 5

Think about all the different kinds of machines you have learned about. What kind of a machine are you most like? Why? How? What do you do? Write the story about you the machine in your MACHINE BOOK. 6